Our Debt to Greece and Rome

EDITORS
GEORGE DEPUE HADZSITS, PH.D.

DAVID MOORE ROBINSON, PH.D., LL.D.

THE GREEK FATHERS

BY

JAMES MARSHALL CAMPBELL

32259

COOPER SQUARE PUBLISHERS, INC.
NEW YORK
1963

Nihil Obstat: ARTHUR J. SCANLAN, S.T.D., *Censor Librorum*

Imprimatur: ✠ PATRICK CARDINAL HAYES, *Archbishop,*
New York

New York, May 2, 1929

Published 1963 by Cooper Square Publishers, Inc.
59 Fourth Avenue, New York 3, N. Y.
Library of Congress Catalog Card No. 63-10279

PRINTED IN THE UNITED STATES OF AMERICA

To

WILLIAM HENRY CAMPBELL

MY FATHER

PREFACE

I HAVE kept to the business of Greek patristic influence almost baldly in the following pages, to an abbreviated statement of what in the West without the Greek Fathers could not have been. So comprehensive a term as "The Greek Fathers" connotes periods as well as persons, and their Western influence stretches far beyond the four countries here taken as typical. Several periods have been treated summarily and many persons and places have been ignored, in an effort to include in this volume's format a minimum representative of each. Martyr-tales and the Christian Apocrypha are a great fact in the time of the Fathers and a force in the after-world; Cyril of Jerusalem and Cyril of Alexandria, Theodoret and Maximus Confessor are major patristic personalities of posthumous Western traces; Spain, Holland, Poland, and Belgium deserve place in a detailed study. All these have been deliberately sacrificed to this volume's peculiar purpose — the suggestion, by typical examples, of the fact and career of influence exerted by the Greek Fathers in that Western world which became so estranged from their own.

I wish here to acknowledge my debt to the following kind colleagues: to Dr. M. R. P. McGuire, for a searching review of the manuscript; to Professor P. J. Healy, for valuable bibliographical suggestions; to Professor R. J. Deferrari and the Rev. L. L. McVay for a careful review and criticism. My thanks are also due to my friend M. Jean Malye of the Association Guillaume Budé for valuable bibliographical suggestions.

J. M. CAMPBELL

CONTENTS

CHAPTER		PAGE
	Preface	vii
I.	Introductory	3
II.	The Greek Fathers; their Chief Representatives	19
III.	The Fourth and Fifth Centuries	85
IV.	From the Fifth through the Fifteenth Century	93
V.	High Renaissance and the Reform of Ecclesiastical Learning	109
VI.	The Seventeenth and Eighteenth Centuries	121
VII.	The Nineteenth Century . . .	132
VIII.	Conclusion	146
	Notes	159
	Bibliography	163

THE GREEK FATHERS

THE GREEK FATHERS

I. INTRODUCTORY

ON THE shelves of any representative university library stretches the Migne collection of the Greek and Latin Fathers. It is not a complete assembly of all that the Fathers wrote. It is not a complete assembly of all that remains of them, but most of what does remain is here in the crowded, small-type pages of nearly four hundred large octavos — to overwhelm the curious onlooker with a sense of awful vastness. The Greek portion of this mighty deposit bulks to one hundred and sixty-six numbers (eighty-one, if minus the parallel Latin translation), heavy with the mental labors of thirteen centuries of theology. It is of varying degrees of literary excellence and of varying degrees of originality. But somehow what is here has escaped the wastage of time. Enough has been thought of its component members to preserve them from the attrition that has ruined so much of antiquity. And even the uninstructed observer of these tall octavos must see here an influence in the world, may conjecture that traces of that influence may be actual even now.

Only a few of these volumes concern us here and only the first seven of these thirteen centuries. Important as were others for their own age and place, the totality of Greek patristic influence may be summed up in a few great men — creative men themselves or at least representative in their own achievement of what their lesser brethren did, of sufficient authority in their own and after-times to direct the channels of patristic effort in the East and to bridge the gulf between the East and that West which shares Our Debt to Greece and Rome. By the end of the fifth century of our era most of these men were dead, living only in the compilations of their numerous disciples and imitators. For reasons that will appear hereafter St. John of Damascus must be included in their number and we therefore conclude the patristic period only with his death in the middle of the eighth century. The writers in the Migne who flourished after St. John's death, even as most in the three centuries before it, are but echoes

INTRODUCTORY

of what had gone before them.[1] When we refer to a period of originality of seven centuries, therefore, we imply many lacunae, and when we add the test of appreciable influence on the West, many more writers fall away. The misfortunes which have come to Greek and the Greek Fathers in the march of the centuries afford the presentation of the outlines of so vast a subject as their influence on the West in so small a compass. The individual contacts with the West were very few; the contributions of the rest can be presented as of one man. These circumstances are the accident which makes possible this little book. They in no wise minimize the fact that the influence of the Greek Fathers in the West has been a profound and enduring one.

At the outset we face a problem of nomenclature. What do we mean by "Fathers"? Chronologically the question is exactly and easily answered in so far as the Greek Orient is concerned. We have the approval of historians both of literature and theology and philosophy in reducing Migne's thirteen centuries to seven, in dating the Greek Middle Ages from the death of St. John of Damascus. But if we would construct a canon of the Fathers — a

[5]

list of names acceptable to all who have a professional interest in the subject — we are predestined to failure. The theologian cannot accept as a "Father" a writer who, beyond his witness and work in dogma, did not live in orthodox communion with the Church and whose life was not eminent for sanctity. And yet there are a number of authors, unorthodox in some points, and a number certainly not eminent for sanctity, whose works nevertheless belong by title of content to the contemporary Christian literature. Because of this title the historian of literature cannot cast them out. He must either call them "Fathers" to the disturbance of his sense of the appropriate or find the noncommittal term which will include them. Now this second alternative is not open to us here. In a popular work we must use the popular term that has been sanctioned by the usage of centuries. For us, then, the "Fathers" are the ecclesiastical writers from the late first to the middle eighth century.[2] Fortunately for our sense of the fitness of things, however, there is no man whom we must treat individually who is not a "Father" in a sense that will be approved by all. This is not to say that formal heretics, for instance,

INTRODUCTORY

did not exert in their negative way an enormous influence by the exaggerations for which they fought, but that the severely orthodox West did not finally accept their doctrines. What they did belongs to the general make-up of their times so far as this book is concerned and what influence they had finds lodgement in the West lost in the definitions of orthodoxy.

Greek patristic literature arrives at the full stature of productive maturity at about the time that the Church emerges from her three centuries' outlawry — from about the Peace of Constantine in 313. From then until near the end of the fifth century is a truly golden age — a period of mighty controversy among great minds on matters of unique importance. The literature which arises from this supreme effort of singular talent, both in the excellence of its content and for the most part in the perfection of its form, crowns the preparatory work of the centuries preceding and serves as the model for the inferior centuries which follow. Most of the Fathers whose individual traces can be found in the West live in this fourth and fifth century heyday. To this period therefore we devote most attention. But in any survey of influences a period of preparation cannot be ignored, and a period of decadence may produce men to whom talent or accident assigns a rôle in the life of the after-world. Origen, at least, from the period of preparation, and St. John Damascene, from the period of decline, must find a place in any summary.

The literature of these seven centuries is a unit in its purpose — the service of Christianity. But this service finds expression in a variety of literary forms drawn from the world in which Christianity grew, called to a new career by the exigencies of the early church. Some of these forms are ultimately Jewish, most of them are actually Hellenic, even when Jewry is their immediate source. When we mention Jewish originals, we do not refer to the older, Israelitic literature that antedated the closing of the Old Testament canon. This was a literature of marvelous fertility in the invention of vehicles for the expression of its feelings and thought, but of itself it gave none of them to Christianity. Whatever literary frames the Church of the Fathers owes to Jewish literature, she owes to the extra-canonical, hellenized literature, particularly from the first century B.C. to the Talmudic beginnings of the second century of our era. And thus the parable, the

INTRODUCTORY

religious song, the allegory, perhaps, and probably the exegetical homily — so familiar to readers of the Fathers — bear testimony to the specifically Jewish element in the contacts of the early church. But it is in Hellenism directly that we must seek the source of most patristic forms.

Here we must be cautious, however, even if we cannot be precise. There is an enthusiasm in some of us, inherited from Renaissance ancestors and abetted by phil-hellenists of the last century, to impose a purely Greek paternity on whatever comes into the modern world not innocent of the impress of Greece. And there is a tendency abroad in the world today, which derives from this same irreverent century, to reduce the cultural constituents of a given epoch simply and solely to types that precede in time, to brand as a contact what may frequently be only a coincidence. It was once the doctrine of Classical Scholarship that classical Roman literature is but a reproduction in the Latin tongue, with certain concessions to Roman manners, of Greek originals. The doctrine may still be fashionable but it is no longer orthodox. For a quarter of a century now Classical Scholarship has been doing penance for one of the sins of her phil-hellenism, in a large and increasing literature devoted to the originality of the Romans. What scholarship has done for pagan Rome, it must still do in a large way for early Christianity. And while we cannot be precise about it always, in lieu of investigations still to be made, we can state the fact whose details become daily clearer. The Greek Fathers are of the unity of Hellenism, certainly, as we shall see hereafter, but they are no mere echo, even in their forms, of the Greek literature that had gone before them. Up to the beginning of the second century of our era, the Greek literary forms are either absent or are suggested so faintly that nothing can be made of the fact. One will search the Apostolic Fathers in vain for even that scanty evidence of Hellenic forms which would give a phil-hellenist comfort. Gradually, inevitably, these forms take their place in the literature of the expanding church, but only as refashioned by the church's practical aims, a church which even in the second century had her guiding traditions. And while in the apology and the dialogue, the chronicle and the history, the treatise and the legend, the didactic poem and the dramatic poem, the biography

INTRODUCTORY

and the eulogy, we recognize undoubted Hellenic originals, we cannot but perceive them altered by the conditions of their new career. And we may assume as much for the epic, the tragedy, and the comedy, which in their Christian dress have vanished. Christianity was something new under the sun, new in thought, in spiritual content, with new needs, dominated by one over-mastering purpose. Even the most atticistic of the Fathers was sobered by that purpose; even in the forms of literature used by him he shows the effects of its arresting presence.

And he shows it in all phases of his heritage from antiquity. Scholars of our time admit the Fathers as an integral part of Greek literature from the second century on. They see in the infiltration of Greek thought and forms into Christian literature a new operation of the Greek spirit. Some of them may see too much, but all of them point to many details in support of their contentions. If, for the sake of comparison, we contrast the Christian and pagan streams at the height of their resemblance — in the fourth and fifth centuries — we observe striking differences that were even more striking in the less friendly epochs which had preceded. Between pagans contemporary with the Fathers and the Fathers themselves stood the career and cross of Christ, the doctrine of the kingdom which is not of this world, those traditions of other-worldliness which grew from this doctrine in the Apostolic Age and conditioned every age that followed, and that now three centuries after the death of Our Saviour, even in the full tide of a revived Hellenism, were imposing limits on that revival. This other-world element is often hidden in the theological strife of the fourth century. Sometimes we seem to have the full force of the later Hellenism with us again in the sophistic display of rhetorical device, the elaborate and subtle and abusive exercise of the reason, but not even thus for long. The fundamental differences between Hellenism and Christianity soon become evident even in the most literal Christian disciple of the Second Sophistic. This-worldliness versus other-worldliness seems to be the root of the matter, the test that differentiates in all the interchanges. The conquest of Alexander the Great and the later absolutism of Rome had qualified the career of Hellenism itself in ways that need not be detailed here. When we speak of Hellenism divorced from the added traits of a particular time and place, purified of the grosser strata that cling to any movement in this world, of the Hellenism that endures amid all the changes, we speak of something that despite the flights of its loftiest philosophers is strictly confined to this earth and that in its highest codes of morality finds here its sanction; a belief in the sovereign importance of this world's affairs and in the legitimacy of aspiring to leadership therein, a confidence in the sufficiency of the reason and the willingness to follow wherever it may lead, the enjoyment of the beauty of this world and of all sensible beauty, the habit of trying everlastingly to see the world as it is. In the singularly gifted race from whom it sprang, it had issued in an achievement of originality of thought which marked the lines of future development and in a literary art of unapproachable excellence. And while now in the fourth century, and before, it had descended for the most part to a generation of pagans weak in creative power and of a taste that was tawdry and degenerate and of opportunities limited by external conditions, it was still Hellenism which was operating in its abiding characteristics.

THE GREEK FATHERS

Essentially Christianity was and is the contrary of this. The development of Christian literature reveals a continuous approach to the Hellenic, of course. The more Christianity expanded, the more frequently the disciples of pagan Hellenism were found among her followers, the more was her further expansion conditioned, humanly speaking, by the appropriation of Hellenic elements. But it was not so in the beginning, and it was never so essentially. The literature of the Greek Fathers, even in its later phases, enjoyed uninterrupted continuity with that of the Apostolic Age. Its earliest efforts were contemporary with the end of the Sub-apostolic Age. For several decades Christianity was either quite ignorant of Hellenism, with some notable exceptions like St. Luke, or hostile to it. To write in a given tongue is not to be wholly independent of the traditions which it carries, and it would be a mistake to suppose that the stratum of society in which Christianity first spread was entirely unaffected by the cultural strata above it. But it was a scanty influence, with rarest exceptions, so scanty as to be unrecognized by those whom it touched, and something to be assumed from the laws of literary development rather than

INTRODUCTORY

assessed. This earliest literature was not consciously literature. The first writers, in emphatic consistency with their other-world viewpoint, almost unanimously treated language with indifference. One wrote because of some practical urge in the contemporary church. Writing was but an unavoidable substitute on occasion for oral tradition. Therefore one wrote, but with no design of art and with no consciousness of participating in a literature which afterwards would be cherished. These earlier communities thought themselves cut off from the Greek world in things of the spirit by a belief which looked away from class-distinctions and above national prejudices and beyond the borders of the earth to the Unseen and by a knowledge sharply differentiated from the wisdom of this world. In this earlier time, before the influx of Hellenism began to complicate the prospect, these abiding notes of Christianity stood out clearly — a belief in the secondary importance of things of earth, detachment from this world's concerns, pious certitude and joyous expectation of the life hereafter, compassion for the great masses of mankind, the submission of reason to authority when authority finally spoke, the beauty of humility — all these flowed from the personality of Our Saviour and from that otherworldliness which is His doctrine. These were marks never to be obscured in all the assimilations of Christianity expanding into the surrounding Hellenism.

If Hellenism is one thing and Christianity is another, the Greek Fathers are of the unity of Hellenism nevertheless. When we use the term "Christian Hellenism" we are not attempting a paradox. We mean that the old Hellenic civilization finds a new lease of life, a circumscribed life, a life minus the principle of indiscriminate liberty of the reason, for instance — but yet life and growth, as distinguished from decay and final death in its pagan haunts. The principal force of Christianity comes from elsewhere, most of its ideas and sentiments are non-Hellenic, but Hellenism contributed ideas too, and above all it contributed its literary art and its intellectual method. When we speak of the Greek Fathers in literary history, we do not think primarily of the earliest, extra-canonical authors who happened to write in Greek, as the Apostolic Fathers did, but of writers from the second century on increasingly penetrated with the Hellenic spirit, writers whose claim to distinction in after-times rests chiefly upon the presence of that spirit in themselves, in their contemporaries, and, after the first century, in their predecessors. For without the spirit of Hellenism the theological problems of the second and following centuries would scarcely have arisen and made these Fathers, armed with this spirit against the results of its own curiosity, the instruments of orthodoxy, even as the content of Hellenism — its Greek philosophy — furnished the intellectual frames wherein orthodoxy placed the faith for after-times. Without Hellenism there would have been no golden age of Patristic literature, as we conceive it on its literary side — no Basil, no Chrysostom, no Gregory of Nazianzus. There would still have been eloquence, since eloquence is an endowment of nature; there would still have been dialectics as learned from the Jewish doctors; there would still have been historiography of a kind and problems to perplex the mind; there would still have been some faint, unconscious heritage of Hellenism derived from the hellenized Judaism of the first century B.C., but there would have been neither the finish of form, the richness of resource, the rational method, the patience of labor, the boldness of speculation, that are of the very spirit of Greece, and there would not have been that fecundity of production which even in its fragments stretches so impressively before us in the Migne on our library shelves. These suppositions, these might-have-beens, imply a world become suddenly static, a Chinese Wall cutting off Christians from the rest of the race, a disobedience of the Church of the Fathers to Our Saviour's command to teach all nations, a revocation of the part that Greek and Hellenism were to play in the divine plan. These suppositions are largely idle, as they are historically absurd, if they do not serve to bring home to us something of the tremendous fact of Hellenism in the life of Christianity; if they do not emphasize the fact that the Greek Fathers are of the unity of Hellenism, and that a survey of their influence in the West is a survey of just another portion of Our Debt to Greece and Rome.

II. GREEK FATHERS; THEIR CHIEF REPRESENTATIVES

WHEN you turn for the first time to the *Index Nominum* of your first manual of patrology, you will be astounded at the multitude of terms there, new to your experience. Wide reading has made you cautious against anticipating details of the unknown, but it has scarcely prepared you for the near half-thousand strangers which such an *Index* displays. Greek names and Latin names, Syrian, Arabian, and Coptic; Armenian names, Ethiopian names, Spanish, Gallic, and Gothic; orthodox names, heretic names, great names and little; false names and true names and titles to works anonymous — they are ghosts and fragments now, for the most part; the last traces in many instances of men almost forgotten, but still telling of a productivity in the Early Church that stretched from the Pillars of Hercules to the Persian Gulf and from the banks of the Rhine to near the Nile's sources. The Greek Fathers were the fountain and center, after the Gospel, of this productivity. From them finally proceeded to men of other tongues the ideas, the problems, the solutions first formulated in Greek. They proceeded in translation ultimately; in the beginning they proceeded in Greek. For about the first three centuries of her life the Church had in Greek a universal language. Her Greek-speaking communities were in all the considerable cities of both East and West. Towards the end of the second century Tertullian began to struggle with Latin as a medium for Christian ideas, but in him the substance of doctrine is wholly Greek, as in the Latin Fathers generally until Augustine's time, and even the great Augustine leaned heavily on Hellenic predecessors. In these facts we have already a foretaste of the Greek Fathers in the West, of the men whose tongue for so long was the medium of writing there, whose works thus nourished beginnings which come through the Middle Ages to us.

From the early years of the second century we date the visible beginnings of Christian Hellenism, and we are already in the midst of a group of writings and writers[3] extending halfway across the century who are apart from

GREEK FATHERS

that Hellenism. The Apostolic Fathers were of great authority in the Early Church because of their proximity to the Apostles, but lacking, as they did, that preciseness and elegance of diction which Hellenism would have given them, they were destined to increasing oblivion as the spirit of Hellenism grew and called for dogmatic definition. Ignatius, the most precise and colorful, escaped the fullness of their general fate, his works turning up now and again even in medieval Latin collections. In the theological strife which followed so closely the revolt of Luther and his associates, these witnesses to the practice of the Primitive Church came to life in many editions, and down to the present day they are of primary importance in the various interests of theology because of their unique chronological advantage among extra-canonical books. They are outside the stream of Hellenism, however, and therefore outside the scope of this chapter.

THE APOLOGISTS

All ancient Christian literature is affected by apologetic tendencies and no small part of it from first to last could be assigned to the apologetic *genre,* but, by one of those curious imprecisions of nomenclature so frequent in patristic science, the word apologist has been preëmpted by the first conscious mediators between Hellenism and Christianity. The Greek Apologists,[4] who stretch over the second and the beginnings of the third century, take their name from the common motive of their literary career — the defense of Christianity against the persecutions of slander evoked by the Church's expansion. In discourse, satire and dialogue, epistle, apology and treatise, they vary the form of their protagonism, revealing thus the pagan training which most of them had received. Of the twelve or more writers belonging to the group, five are lost entirely or survive only in fragments. Melito, bishop of Sardis, was among these — a great figure in his day, of broad mind and many activities, the loss of whose works is one of the major regrets of modern patristic scholarship. Of the survivors Justin Martyr alone rises clearly above mediocrity.

The Apologists did enduring work despite endowments generally slender. Regardless of the measure of immediate success which attended their principal objective, in them are the beginnings of Patristic Philosophy, the first attempts to justify Christianity to the pagan world on the grounds of reason. Such attempts required of course the employment of that formal logic which pagan Greeks had developed, but they did not imply the "Hellenization of Christianity," in the phrase of some enthusiasts. It was a revelation interpreted by reason which the Apologists presented to contemporaries, but it was first and foremost a revelation. They borrowed heavily and at times inappropriately from the pagan resources at hand, but they were basically and thoroughly Christian. In the second century of our era the dominant philosophy was penetrated with the religious spirit, and it was no small advantage to the missionary church that its doctrines were presented in philosophical dress, but between the Divine Word, the source of truth for the Apologists, and the interior daemon of individual reason which guided men like Epictetus and Marcus Aurelius, was the wide gulf that separated religion from philosophy. The Apologists were in the direct line of descent of Christian tradition. With them began a process of accommodation, inevitable in the progress of the Church, between

THE GREEK FATHERS

Christianity and the dominant philosophy, a process carried on with greater skill and knowledge by the Alexandrian doctors of the third century and issuing finally in the fourth century in the comprehensive Faith of Nicaea and a Christianization of Hellenism rather than a "Hellenization of Christianity." With the Fathers of the following epochs the Apologists are not to be compared in cultural attainment or positive influence, but they were the necessary preliminaries to those more brilliant periods and much that they did found lodgement there. And among them Justin and Tatian and Melito laid their late contemporary, Tertullian, under heavy debt — a channel by no means small for direct penetration of the West.

Melito, the talented bishop of Sardis, was possibly the greatest of the Greek Apologists. Justin Martyr is certainly the most important among those still extant. Born a pagan and become a pagan philosopher, Justin found his way to Christianity, like St. Augustine after him, over the bridge of Platonic idealism. His apologetic purpose discovered that Christianity and Greek philosophy were really related. In both was the Logos: a potential logos in paganism; the fullness and perfection of Christ, the Logos, in Christianity. In pagan philosophy was part of the truth discovered after much pain and doubt according to the portion of the Logos granted to it; in Christianity was the whole of the truth. Both had in common definite doctrines, but Christianity possessed certain higher truths made all the more secure by Revelation. This discovery of common ground between paganism and Christianity was a far cry from the Apostolic Church but an inevitable development of the Apostolic mission. This emphasis on superiority rather than contrariety, this assertion of a doctrine lofty enough to include and pass beyond the best that paganism could offer was a powerful polemic in its own day and an example to the ages which followed. Here is the first serious examination, extant to us, of the relations between faith and reason. This distinction is not a mere matter of quantity, as Justin's successors were to show, but the pursuance of his thesis through all its logical implications was preliminary to the clarity which they achieved.

THE GREEK FATHERS

St. Irenaeus

From before the Christian era — how long before is not yet determined — there came out of the non-Greek East, apparently, to mingle with Hellenic and Jewish religion, that curious and variant response to the problem of evil which goes under the collective name of the Gnosis. There is no defining Gnosticism, so many were its sects and so contradictory their tenets and so flagrant their borrowings both of ideas and phraseology from the religions which it met in its wanderings, but through all the confusion of its luxuriant systems ran the fundamental note of pessimism — the conviction apparently original with itself that matter is a deterioration of the spirit, that the universe is the principle of evil and therefore uncreated by and in opposition to the Deity. Salvation for the Gnostic consisted in the possession of knowledge, in the vision of the divinity that came from direct mystical relationships with God and in which magic formulae somehow had place. This is undoubtedly very vague, but so is Gnosticism in the scanty remains of its once great literature. Basically neither Hellenic nor Christian, this strange syncretism interests us here because, with cancer-like facility of adaptation, it finally fastened on Christianity and, appropriating its nomenclature, Christology, sacraments even, paraded plausibly before the unlearned as Christianity's better self.

St. Irenaeus has other claims to after-world attention than his refutation of the Gnosis. Although Gnosticism lingered on into the fifth century, he inaugurated its long decline, and within fifty years of his own death the Gnosis was visibly crumbling. This were a great performance for any man; something to be grateful for, could we only appreciate now how menacing once was the Gnosis. Work incidental to his Gnostic polemic, however, is a more tangible source of his fame.

Born in or near the Asiatic Greek city of Smyrna in the third decade of the second century, he died the bishop of Lyons in Gaul during the opening years of the third, illustrating by the circumstances of these termini and by his cosmopolitan career meanwhile the ready union which then existed between the churches of the East and the West. He lived in a time of transition. As a boy he had listened to St. Polycarp, who had been a disciple of St. John.

His early and middle life paralleled the age of the Apologists. His declining years were contemporary with Clement's presidency at Alexandria. He is the last recorded student of the personal pupils of the Apostles; he was the first great systematic expositor of the faith which the Apostles bequeathed. He did not work out a science of theology. He had not the philosophic penetration which such a feat supposes. He was not a speculative pioneer. His was the first extended exposition of the content as distinguished from the facts of Revelation. In that exposition, under the stimulus of a polemical purpose, certain central tenets of Christian belief — the Incarnation, the Redemption, the Eucharist, the Mass, the Resurrection of the Body — came to the foreground of discussion; certain principles of theological procedure were launched on an active career; a theory of authoritative Catholicism was given, of the Church as a teaching institution, of the primacy of the Pope, of the mechanism of post-Apostolic Revelation. There was scarcely an element of his theory, as there was not a principle enunciated, which did not go back to the days of the Apostles, which is not found obscurely or explicitly in Irenaeus' predecessors. This was not creative work, but it was necessary work and work possible of production only by a high intelligence. Content to be a witness to the Apostolic Faith, he was forced by the threat of a deadly heresy to expound that faith with an elaboration and a display of synthetic power which not only crushed Gnosticism but which gave to the scientific theology born in his last years the substance and the spirit it has possessed ever since. From Tertullian Western theology was to borrow its technical language — to clothe the materials which Irenaeus transmitted. Through the School of Alexandria it was to become a science — and tread the path of Tradition which Irenaeus marked out.

Through the rôle which theology has played since his time, the work of Irenaeus is felt in every age. On the morrow of his death St. Hippolytus and Tertullian add their personal borrowings from him to the general debt of the West, and in times of theological crisis recourse is had to his *Adversus Haereses*, in the Latin version upon which now we must mainly depend. In the eighteenth-century West even forgeries were made under his name to further the cause of Pietistic theology. In the nine-

THE GREEK FATHERS

teenth century and down to a late date a battle has raged around the testimony of his extant works, for he joins as does no other Father the times of the Apostles with the beginnings of Christian theology.

Until the last decades of the second century the leading figures of Ecclesiastical Literature come from Asia Minor and Syria, and all of them write in Greek, whether resident in the East or the West. Thereafter the leading figures no longer come exclusively from Asia Minor and Syria, and many of them write in Latin. In the West, Latin is not clearly in the ascendant until the middle of the third century, but already at the close of the second century it is the literary medium of North Africa. The Greek Fathers in the realm of thought will continue to nourish the West, but more and more through translations. The Empire's universal language is withdrawing into the East. The world of the original patristic tongue is narrowing. We must be conscious now of a Latin literature growing in territory and importance, as St. Hippolytus must have been conscious of it in Rome near the middle of the third century, when he put forth in Greek the last extant patristic work in that language written by a Western man.

In the last decades of the second century there emerges from the obscurity which hides the earlier Alexandrian church the famous Catechetical School of that city. The rise of the school seems sudden to us now because of the perfection of its structure and the intelligence of its method when first we know it intimately — a perfection which argues a development reaching back to the early years of the century and stirred to rapid progress, perhaps, by the constant menace of the Gnosis. The perpetuity of the school is assured by a regular succession of teachers. Its effectiveness is attained by a definite objective and an adequate method. It aims to organize scientifically the deposit of the Faith, and among the preparatory studies given its pupils are a thorough study of Greek philosophy and a systematic introduction to the method of allegorical interpretation. With this is combined thus early a training to the life of asceticism — a propaedeutic for theological excellence which the experience of the future was to approve. For five centuries now Alexandria had been the world's intellectual rendezvous, the source and center of that cosmopolitan Hellenism which had prepared the way for the Gospel. Here, in the erudite city of the Ptolemies, whence the wisdom of the Old Law had passed through Septuagint translators to the knowledge of pagan peoples, the doctrines of the New Law enter the learned world in their first theological setting. For near a century and a half and in a Christian rôle Alexandria is again preeminent.

This is not the greatest period of the Greek patristic. Its Golden Age is not yet. In literary grace, St. Methodius possibly excepted, the Latin writers of the contemporary West are on the whole superior. It is a time which in influence, however, yields place to none.

We have seen in the preceding century occasional overtures to pagan Hellenism. Justin had exaggerated even in his efforts at reconcilement. But the older tradition of hostility, encouraged by the Gnosis in its Greek dress, was still the prevailing attitude. Even among friends of Hellenism, the relation of the latter to Christianity had yet to be worked out clearly. The solution of this problem — practically the enlistment of Greek culture in the cause of the Gospel — is the first of Alexandria's services to the Church. This solution did not crush anti-hellenism among Christians; it will be with us again in the Golden Age, but what had been done hitherto with hesitation or half-consciously by the Greek Fathers was now done boldly and with full intelligence. Christian thought had not only to be clothed in the grace of form that was Hellenism. It must also show itself capable of extended conceptions, vast and fecund syntheses, systems as comprehensive as the pagan Greeks had produced. The whole apparatus of pagan culture must be devoted to an anti-pagan purpose. The isolated and groping tendencies of the second century now grew into a program, so to speak, and Clement of Alexandria was the first to formulate it.

Clement of Alexandria

Clement, as no other Father before him, stands out from the pages of his writings a man of flesh and blood. Heretofore, the note of self-obliteration had prevailed in the works of the Fathers. Writing was an occasional thing; something to be tolerated, in contrast to pagan literary manners, only for an impersonal end — the interests of the Gospel.

Even pagan converts had felt the force of this tradition. Lesser figures are lost in this pious subordination, and even Ignatius and Justin and Irenaeus come before us dimly. Christian literature in the new period loses nothing of its singleness of purpose, but its effort to realize this purpose is more extensive and the men it enlists are on the whole greater minds. They cling with all their might to the tradition of other-worldliness, but in the execution of the more elaborate tasks which their own time imposes, they write unconsciously into their more voluminous, more comprehensive works the record of their personalities. Clement is the first of these, setting down next to nothing about himself directly, but revealing in his discussions of knowledge, matrimony, the state, and the many other questions which could not escape treatment in his writings the outlines of a very attractive personality — of great personal austerity, but with a large-minded view of the universe, of broad culture, gentle and tolerant.

Born in Athens, seemingly of pagan parents, he had come to Alexandria and its Catechetical School, after extensive travels, to sit at the feet of Pantaenus. In the last years of the second century he was an ordained priest, Pantaenus' associate in the direction of the School, and after the latter's death around the year 200 was alone in its presidency. In Clement the spirit of Justin is again alive, to put Greek speculation at the service of Christian belief — and the method of the Greek Gnosis is adapted in a sense — the attempt to advance from belief to knowledge, although Christianity is the norm of such advance as Clement made. He is the author, among many other works, of a famous and eccentric trilogy still extant, which presents with a mastery hitherto unknown the wealth of Christian ideas. So vast a subject would lose nothing from exposition in attractive dress, and Clement leads by easy and pleasant stages from one consideration to another. After a hortatory discourse (*Protrepticus*) to the Greeks, which is really an apology and a philippic, he instructs (*Paedagogus*) the converted reader in the new life of grace and truth. Here we should expect the initiated Christian to be guided through Christian dogma (which will come only with Origen). Instead he is introduced to a miscellany (*Stromata*) of treatises on various subjects connected with the life of a true Christian. Much has been said for and against the formlessness of the trilogy in its later parts and of the uneven quality of its style; of contradictions, obscurities, and errors of fact; of the display of an erudition borrowed from convenient florilegia. And much can be said of theological incorrectness here and there in the work, of the too great reliance on knowledge, even though it be knowledge of religion. But these are the marks of a first attempt, revealing on the historical as on the theological side the novelty of the effort to adjust them frankly. There is no denying his grasp of much pagan philosophy and literature, nor the correctness of his principles on the relations of faith and knowledge. And while he leaves no system, for he lacks the synthetic power, the attempt he made is the important thing, the audacious attempt as it seems to us, and of a significance scarcely to be exaggerated, for with it the philosophic spirit enters frankly into the service of Christian doctrine and with it begins, however awkwardly and blunderingly, the theological science of the future.

In the history of pedagogy Clement's trilogy is likewise a landmark. Combining pagan and Christian studies, it does not abandon the contention of the Apologists that education for the next life is superior. It does recognize, however, the importance of secular culture during one's earthly sojourn, and constructs, therefore, a hierarchy of studies in which the secular sciences are propaedeutic to the lofty study of Christianity. In thus subordinating secular knowledge to the service of religious instruction Clement suggests a motive for use of the Classics, effective in their preservation. And he inaugurates a theory which has a long chapter in the history of pedagogy.

He has still another title to enduring fame in that he was the teacher, one of the teachers, of Origen.

Origen

Born in Egypt and apparently in Alexandria in 185 or 186, Origen so impressed the contemporaries even of his youth with the splendor of his gifts and erudition that at eighteen years of age he was chosen to succeed Clement in the presidency of the Alexandrian School. Into the less than seventy years of his life he crowded an amount of writing and instructing and preaching that even without the distractions of his considerable travelling is beyond our comprehension. Even when we take account of his seven and more stenographers and his corps of clerks and other assistants and make whatever we can of his hasty and even slovenly style, we are still bewildered by the eight hundred titles attributed to him in St. Jerome. He made journeys to Rome and Arabia during his earlier years. In 215 he spent some time in Caesarea of Palestine, incurring the displeasure of his bishop by preaching there, though not yet in proper orders. About 230 he again went to Caesarea and was raised to the priesthood without the permission of his bishop. Banished from Alexandria in consequence, he made Caesarea the seat of a new school that became famous through the nearer Orient. Journeys to Africa and Arabia and possibly the persecution of Maximin the Thracian interrupted his intense productivity. Otherwise he was ceaselessly active in Caesarea until caught up in the Decian Persecution. Enjailed and tortured then, he never recovered his former vigor and the industry which it supported, and died soon after his release, in the sixty-ninth year of his age.

Origen, like the city of his childhood, was a cosmopolitan. He touched the principal cities of East and West in the contacts of his career; he possessed all the learning of his time. He is one of the most voluminous writers of antiquity, the greatest scholar of the Early Church, the greatest theologian of the East, the first great pulpit-orator. Text Criticism, Exegesis, Apologetics, Dogmatic Theology, Metaphysics, Asceticism — he did superlative work in all of these and he did much besides. He achieved the union of Greek Philosophy and Christianity, for which Clement had prepared the way and thus constructed the first summa of Theology ever to be organized in the Church. And he thereby gave ecclesiastical studies a new dignity among the sciences. From his own time, whatever is to be made of the fact, the best thought and literature of the West have been either Christian or deeply influenced by Christianity. During his life-time his renown was universal; his ideas circulated through influential pupils, his writings travelled through the empire. On the morrow of his death he was the arsenal for more than one party in the great Trinitarian controversy. To name the great men influenced by him down to the end of the fourth century is to call the roll of leading minds in both East and West.

The weakness of Origen as a theologian was the weakness of Clement before him—the over-emphasis of knowledge, the leaning too heavily on philosophy. His system was developed on the basis of Greek speculation rather than on the basis of the Gospel. Three great doctrines in Origen's system—the eternal creation of the world, the pre-existence of the soul, the final restoration of all intelligent creatures to God's friendship—are echoes of Platonic and Neo-Platonic philosophy in points fundamentally un-Christian, reducing as they do salvation to a cosmic process and destroying thereby divine as well as human freedom. It is no cause for wonderment therefore that the Church did not consider Origen's system a satisfactory synthesis of Christianity and pagan philosophy, though it is doubtful that he was ever condemned by the Church. The Platonic Idealism in which Origen had been educated began to lose its patristic vogue towards the end of the fifth century. Aristotelian Realism was supplanting it. This gave impetus to an anti-Origenist movement which had arisen within a century of Origen's death and which was based partly on Origen's errors, partly on vague statements in his works, and partly on personal disputes between protagonists and antagonists, with which Origen had only accidental connection. In the sixth century Justinian condemned Origen to the ruin of his reputation in the East, but not before he had nourished the most venerated Eastern doctors and assured himself an enduring though anonymous life in their works. His name was a byword, however, throughout the Byzantine Middle Ages.

The West was more kind to him. His writings continued to be studied, readings from him were placed in the Roman Breviary; Bede and Bernard respected him. Even through the cloud that passed over his name he exercised a strange fascination. His salvation was a question of the Schools in the fifteenth century. Erasmus in the sixteenth century was enthusiastically in his debt, not hesitating to assert, despite the far-flung preeminence of St. Augustine, that " plus me docet Christianae philosophiae unica Origenis pagina quam decem Augustini."[5] His influence was felt in the seventeenth century in the Quietism of Fénelon and Madame de Guyon.[6] Directly and indirectly, comprehended and misinterpreted, he is the founder of theology and, all things con-

THE GREEK FATHERS

sidered, the most influential of the Greek Fathers. We shall meet greater literary artists in our survey of the Greek Fathers and men with a greater personal following in the West. We shall not meet a greater individual force.

No statement of Origen's influence, however hurried, can ignore his contribution to historiography. In common with most of antiquity he had no interest in history for its own sake, and typically of the Early Church he had no interest in it even as a record of human events. His view-point was theological and otherworldly. The events of this world intrigued his scholarship only for their relations to the next. But since Christ is the Messiah expected of the Jews and the saviour of all mankind, His place in Jewish history and in the history of the world had to be established historically in the face of pagan polemics. In attacking this twofold problem, Origen, the theologian and exegete, affected the subsequent development of historiography. Vital to the historical demonstration of Our Saviour's Messianic character and of Christianity as a fulfillment of Judaism was the consistency between the prophecies of the Old Testament and the narrative of the New. Wrestling with the difficulties presented by an always literal interpretation of the Scriptures, Origen had recourse to the allegorical — a method of exegesis used by both pagans and Jews for centuries as occasion had demanded, wrought into something of a system by his elder contemporary Philo, and found here and there in Christian writers from St. Paul down. Origen applies it as a system to the Scriptures, he theorizes about it, gives it a kind of scientific basis, and employing it in demonstration of the Messianic mission gives it an extension of use hitherto unknown. It thereby entered the science of historiography and offered the only unity to its labors possible in the ancient world by presenting the Messianic Saviour as the central fact of history; it was the source of that Christian philosophy of history which was formally inaugurated by Eusebius, and which meets us much later in Bossuet's *L'histoire universelle* in Louis XIV's time.

EUSEBIUS OF CAESAREA

Eusebius of Caesarea, born within a decade of Origen's death and reared amid the traditions of scholarship which Origen gave to Palestine, chronologically inaugurates the fourth-century literature — the bulk of his writing being done then — but he is more representative of the third. Actually an older contemporary of the earlier fourth-century Fathers, living on and actively into the fourth decade of that century, in the development of Christian literature he is their predecessor, occupied like the generality of third-century Greek Fathers more with ideas than their artistic expression. Of a many-sided literary activity — Bishop Lightfoot names seven distinct departments — he is first and foremost a historian.

Nothing in the appearance of his *Chronicle* suggests to the casual reader its rôle in the History of History. The first part, available for scholarship only within this century, is a source-book of universal history, arranged nation by nation. The second part, known to the West until recently solely through St. Jerome's translation, presents a page with columns of dates down its central portion assembled according to various systems of chronology, these columns being flanked to the right and left by columns of sacred and profane history. Nothing could be more unattractive in appearance than these bald, synchronized annals, and yet they are the model for the chronicles, universal and local, which are in fashion for a thousand years in the West. They present a scheme of ancient chronology which has been accepted almost unaltered down to our day. They marshal the whole panorama of ancient history to show that it was but a preparation for the gospel — a magnificent synthesis, implying an erudition and judgment which are the admiration of modern historians, and a great conception, inherited from Origen and presented here with the simplicity and clarity of a mathematical curve.

The *Ecclesiastical History* is a narrative, of course, but not so much an orderly, logical narrative as a collection of facts and documents, priceless on this score in the general ruin of Christian sources for the first three centuries of our era. Written in its present form on the morrow of the last persecution and in the thick of the Arian controversy, it somehow avoids the bitter spirit of its own time, revealing everywhere in its management of vast reserves of learning a conscientious striving for accuracy and detachment and, amid errors and lacunae inevitable in his day and in the scantiness of his Latin scholarship, splendid critical powers. All ancient historiography, Christian and pagan, is frankly pragmatic rather than scientific, as we understand the latter, and Eusebius is an apologist throughout — a circumstance that makes all the more remarkable the achievement of his objectivity. Beyond the influence which such a work must exert as the first ecclesiastical history, its apologetic view-point is of enormous import in the development of Christian historiography. It presents world-history since the founding of the Church as an unceasing battle between the devil and the kingdom of God; the events of history as so many manifestations of the will of God for his world — a conception characteristic of Christian historiography ever since. Because of this work, chiefly, Eusebius is called the "Christian Herodotus" and the "Father of Church History," and by it he is best known to after-times. Through it and the "Chronicle" Eusebius enjoys an influence in the after-world surpassed only by Origen, Chrysostom, and possibly the Areopagite among the Greek Fathers.

Beginning with the following chapter and continuing through Chapter VI, I restrict the phrase "Greek Fathers" for the most part to the Fathers of the Golden Age, now about to be reviewed in leading representatives. What their predecessors did had the great influence on them suggested in the preceding pages, but that influence, except where specific mention is made to the contrary, reaches the West through the fourth-century and fifth-century Fathers, or through the summary of St. John of Damascus.

The Golden Age

From the Peace of Constantine (313) to the Council of Chalcedon (431) is the Golden Age of the Greek Patristic. In all fields of literature, poetry excepted, the highest perfection was then attained. There were more literary forms employed and they were employed with a mastery which the future could only imitate. The greatest writers of this great time come from Africa and Asia, even as among the contemporary Latin Fathers the African writers are the best. And from a region hitherto scarcely known to literary history, Cappadocia, there suddenly issue writers whose fame endures to the present even beyond the circles of the learned.

The preparatory effort of the second and

third centuries explains in part the preeminence of the fourth. The fourth century happens to be the culmination of a two hundred years' crescendo, the resultant of a long and growing movement that could not cease abruptly. The central fact of the time is the rise of the Church first to the legalized right to existence in Roman society and finally to the privileges and embarrassments of alliance with the state. In the corresponding decline of politico-religious paganism, the old and popular hostility to Hellenic culture loses considerable of its edge; in the consequent influx of converts from paganism, the tradition of hostility is further vitiated. The bold phil-hellenism of the Alexandrian School, so obviously beneficial to Christian exposition and the spread of the Gospel, encourages a host of imitators. The old antihellenism does not die out. In fact it revives again in the West as the Golden Age declines. It is a corollary from the other-worldliness of Christianity inevitable for certain temperaments in any period. But in the fourth century meanwhile pagan culture flourishes in Christian circles as never before, with a resulting literary excellence unapproached hitherto. Almost all the Christian authors of the time had attended sophistic schools and according to the measure of their intellectual endowment reflect the virtues and defects of that training. Some of these defects are in them all, but the most thoroughly sophistic among them are preserved from the monotonous frivolities of their pagan contemporaries by the vital problems and serious purpose of Christianity. And the greater minds are enabled to cast their work in a brilliance of form which is another reason why this age is called " Golden."

A third factor in the greatness of the time is the menace of the heresy of Arianism, the chief concern of the Church and one of the chief concerns of the Empire through the greater part of the century. There is no reconstructing now in its actual circumstance what that battle was, how it stirred the heart and strained the intellect and tore both church and state, enlisting the lungs of unlettered sailors in the war-songs of clashing factions. Sixteen centuries of theological security, which the Golden Age gave the future, dull even the orthodox of our day against the details of that struggle. There is no modern nor medieval parallel to explain its intensity and universality. But when once its central issue is grasped, not even the unorthodox modern smiles at the uproar it provoked. For briefly and humanly speaking, the further life of Christianity waited upon the outcome of that battle. At the very heart of Christianity is the mystery of the Trinity, including among other elements the divinity of the Son and the Holy Ghost. Arianism attacked this mystery, asserting that Christ, the Son of God, was a creature. If Christ were a creature, the worship of Him was idolatry and the full revelation of God to man had not been made.. Polytheism and Platonism and Gnosticism were also implied in various tenets of Arius and his successors. If Arianism had not been crushed, Christianity would have evaporated in time. It is easy for us to see this after the battle; keen, speculative Fathers in the fourth century saw it even before. The first and foremost of these was Athanasius.

St. Athanasius

He was born in Alexandria and for nearly a half-century was Alexandria's bishop, although most of his energies to within a few years of his death must have been absorbed in the synods, banishments, battles with bishops and magistrates and emperors incident to the Arian controversy and his position in it. His voluminous writings — exegetical, apologetical, dogmatic, polemical, disciplinary, moral, epistolary — are connected closely with the master-purpose of his life — the defense of the divinity of Christ. In the realm of thought rather than of literature they wield their influence.

To state Athanasius' position in the Arian controversy is to state his greatest contribution to the future. He was the chief instrument, his was the major rôle, in that conflict which determined that Christianity was to continue. This is the enormous fact impossible of more precise assessment. Great minds and greater literary artists fight in the ranks of orthodoxy, but Athanasius is the leader of them all and the personal inspiration of most. He is a great thinker educated in the culture of the Greek Diaspora and yet he reflects more strikingly than any of his great predecessors that antithesis of pagan thought which is Christianity. He is a thinker but not in the manner of Plotinus and Porphyry, who were sympathetic with all the attempts of the reason and sought everywhere particles of the truth to be united into a system for its own sake. He reflects that new hierarchy of values basic in the most Greek-tempered Christian philosophers which places love above knowledge and religion above philosophy and makes reason ancillary to faith. Hellenic philosophy is ever opening new paths of inquiry and follows wherever they may lead. The Christian philosopher may proceed at will along these same paths, indistinguishable in the details of his method from his pagan contemporary, but his goal is pre-determined, if a crisis arise, because of the primacy of the deposit of the faith in his hierarchy of values and because he is convinced that between what Revelation gives and Reason finds there can be no final clash. This is the difference — and in Athanasius' case it meant the effort to close by a formula all inquiry as to the co-equality of the Son with the Father. It is sometimes said that Athanasius is the founder of a movement which later resulted in the hardening of tradition under Augustine's influence, to the domination of the Church in the Middle Ages. This is to exalt Athanasius as a world-figure and an original force all out of proportion to his deserts. Rather he is the first clear manifestation to us moderns of how Revelation must act when forced by an intellectual crisis to be specific. To have been the leading protagonist of Revelation in such a crisis as was Arianism, however, was to live a career of sovereign importance to the future of civilization.

Aside from his general import in the history of thought, Athanasius exerts a particular influence of wide scope through his *Life of St. Anthony*. Anthony was Coptic rather than Greek, but the Greek-written biography which his life inspired compels his inclusion here. And even apart from the pages of Athanasius, this Egyptian hermit, who may himself have been illiterate in Greek, is one of the most influential figures of the most literary of Christian Greek centuries. Typical of a reaction in his time against the inrush of pagan culture and the false emphasis that so frequently accompanied it, he fled to the desert to escape that culture and inaugurated the movement that was to preserve it. To Anthony more than to any other man must be ascribed the disputed beginnings of Monasticism.[7]

For the generality of aspirants to the life of perfection, Monasticism was the inevitable mode, once the Church had emerged from her outlawry. The relaxation of manners that grew with her growth imperilled ascetical practice in society. Even before the Peace of the Church, virgins were being withdrawn into communities of some sort and the life of ascetics still abroad in the world made for increasing episcopal solicitude. The trial of the last and most severe persecutions urged on the process of withdrawal, and when St. Anthony began the hermit life about 270, anchorites were already on the outskirts of Egyptian villages, living as best they could the other-worldliness of the Gospel. After fifteen such years near his native village, Anthony retired to the desert on the east bank of the Nile, seeking in an abandoned fort uninterrupted approach to God. There was nothing of the pioneer in Anthony's intentions. He was striving only to lead the life of perfection where he himself could live it — in the solitude of the wilderness, where others had lived it before him. But the fame of Anthony spread and other ascetics were driven by the difficulties of their state into the desert wastes and he became a focal point of widespread dissatisfied aspiration. They clustered around his retreat in ever-growing numbers and begged him to come forth and guide them. Finally, about 305, he did come forth from his twenty years' seclusion, to find the surrounding hills covered with the cells of his imitators. For five or six years he ministered to their needs, advising and instructing and organizing them out of the wealth of nearly forty years' experience, thus launching by the drawing-power of his fame, the accident of his charity, and the authority of his sanctity, Christian asceticism in its monastic dress.

Antonian monachism is not the form of monasticism familiar to most of us — the highly-organized community, completely subject to a superior. This form was inaugurated in another part of Egypt by Pachomius, a younger contemporary of St. Anthony. The Antonian variety grew out of the eremetical life which Anthony himself had lived and from such precepts as he had given his disciples. It was the adaptation of the eremetical life to the problem of a colony and even in its largest colonies it remained eremetical — the anchorites living apart from one another in separate cells, bound only to that irreducible minimum of communion and regulation which their juxtaposition and identity of purpose imposed. It spread through Egypt and dominated the East and was the first form recommended to Western imitation, probably through the personal offices of Athanasius. Its introduction there and the Latin translation of the *Life of St. Anthony* occasioned a mighty revival to indigenous Western monasticism and the wide acceptance of the Antonian type itself, although Western needs were finally to hide its impress beneath the more appropriate monachism of St. Benedict.

But its founder and the *Vita* which he inspired have ever played a rôle of influence unhidden. The *Vita Antonii* was the first monk-biography and it unloosed a stream of literature which flows from that day to this. The Lausiac History of Palladius, of first importance in the annals of monachism, and the monastic tales of St. Jerome were two of its earliest off-shoots. A huge literature of edification in the Middle Ages which supplanted in part the older tales of apostles and martyrs draws from the *Vita* its origin. It appears in a famous passage in the *Confessions* of St. Augustine, and was among the last of the literary influences which led to his momentous conversion. " Upon a certain day therefore . . . behold, there came home unto me and Alypius, one Ponticianus, a countryman of ours, an African. . . . He wanted something or other from us; and down together we sat, so that into discourse we fell . . . there began a speech (himself being the relater) of Anthony the monk of Egypt. . . . From this story of Anthony, took he occasion to discourse of the companies of the monasteries. . . . Hereupon took he occasion to tell, how himself . . . and three other of his comrades . . . one afternoon went out to walk into the gardens next the city walls; . . . they stumbled by chance upon a certain little house . . . where they found a little book, wherein the life of Anthony was described. One of them began to read, wonder at it, and to be inflamed with it; and even in the very reading to devise with himself upon the taking such a life upon him . . . and he read on, and was inwardly changed . . . and his mind was quite dispossessed of worldly cares. . . . This was Ponticianus his story. But thou, O Lord, all the while that he was speaking, didst turn me back to reflect upon myself . . . and thou now settedst me before mine own face.

"Thus felt I a corrosive within, yea most vehemently confounded I was with a horrible shame, whenas Ponticianus was a telling that story. And he having done both his tale and the business he came for, went his way, and I into myself. What said I not within myself! With what scourges of condemning sentences lashed I not mine own soul, to make it follow me, endeavoring now to go after thee! And it drew back: it refused, but gave no reason to excuse its refusal by. All its arguments were already spent and confuted. . . ."[8] It was the source of a vast iconography in St. Anthony's honor and of his mighty career as a healer in the Middle Ages.[9] And the theme of the "Temptation of St. Anthony," drawn from the *Vita*, has inspired a huge effort in literature and art down to so late a date as Gustav Flaubert's work of that name.

St. Basil

The primacy in after-world influence shifts, during Anthony's last years, from Alexandria and the desert wastes of Egypt to the mountain country of Cappadocia, and with it shifts the leadership in those discussions which had afforded Egypt her preeminence — the general reconcilement of faith and reason, the problem of Arianism in its post-Nicene phases, the question of Christian humanism, the problem of the perfect life in a fallen world. St. Basil touches all of these problems in a life that would otherwise have been strenuous and for three of them he does work which still endures. He was born about 330, attended the best schools in his native Caesarea, in Constantinople, in Athens, and, thus prepared academically as were only the most cultured men of his time, renounced the brilliant promise of his attainments for the pursuit of monastic asceticism. But new crises in Arianism kept him almost constantly from his monastery, made him the successor of Athanasius in the Arian controversy, and finally elevated him to the Archbishopric of Caesarea and to contests with the imperial throne itself.

Basil comes only after Anthony and Pachomius, however, in the history of monastic beginnings. He was the final architect of monachism as it still obtains through the Orient, and features that seem original with him are among the permanent possessions of the West, such as the common house, the common table, the prayers always in common. And if some or all of these features were to be found in the deserts and mountains before him, the welding of them into a system was his work. He was the first to declare for the superiority of the coenobitical over the anchorite life as the normal form of asceticism. He found a new outlet for monastic effort in good works for one's fellowmen. He reduced the ascetical extravagances of eremetical enthusiasm to the abiding capacity of human nature. Through him monasticism became an institution, something that could live and grow without the capricious appeal of a great personality or the spontaneous ascetical fervor of a particular age and country. He did not write a religious rule, as we understand that term, but he did write "Rules" for living the religious life, which had a wide circulation in Greek, despite the difficulties of their style for later generations, and that in their Latin adaptation by Rufinus were a rich, though minor, source for the Rule of St. Benedict.[10]

Basil was a leader in the Arian struggles long before his episcopal election enlisted him officially. He was not an original theologian, but by his controversial and expository powers and his capacity for prolonged and intense polemics, he became only second to Athanasius in service to Nicene orthodoxy. And he prepared the way by his *De Spiritu Sancto* for the ecumenical decrees on the Holy Ghost which the Council of Constantinople (381) gave to Christian creeds.

No Greek Father save St. Chrysostom is so widely known today and yet the basis of his modern fame was a by-product of his activity. Basil, for all his other concerns and for all that the Alexandrians had done, like most of the Fathers before him, had to face the perennial problem of the Classics. He gave a solution in his tract "To the Youths" which echoes the view-point of Clement of Alexandria, which may have been used by St. Jerome in his apologetic *Epistle LXX,* and may have been a source for St. Augustine in his *De Doctrina Christiana.* It was of great authority at any rate in later ages. We are puzzled at the appeal of an argument which could justify the Classics only as a propaedeutic to the study of the Scriptures, but we can be grateful for it in that it helped to preserve the Classics. To the men of the Early Renaissance Basil's little tract became a vogue and twenty editions of it appeared before 1500. The enthusiasm of the Quattrocento was transmitted to later times. Theologians and philologians celebrated its author in eulogies fulsome and uncritical. It came to the foreground inevitably in battles over the value of the Classics. In our less phil-hellenic and more critical days it has lost much of its currency, but it has still a text-book contact with rising generations.[11]

Its author was more resourceful in action than he was original in thought and yet his work endures in one as in the other, for he brought to ideas and institutions that are still a force in the world a quality of statesmanship that is part of their permanent form. Only St. Chrysostom among the Greek Fathers has influenced the West so tangibly.

St. Gregory of Nyssa

More learned and more profound but less tangibly influential was Basil's younger brother, St. Gregory. In Greek Patristic Philosophy Origen alone is so eminent. He followed in the path of Origen in constructing his system, although with far more of orthodoxy, and like him he sought a rational foundation of the Faith, although with far more of comprehensiveness. No theme intrigued him more than the human knowledge of God and no phase of his philosophical activity interests us more because of its legacy to philosophy and mysticism. He found the possibility of knowing God in man's likeness to Him and an indirect way of thus knowing Him through the order and harmony of His creation. But there is also a direct, mystical way for the soul which can rise above the world of sense and see beyond the testimony of its understanding — an intuitive knowledge, rare and extraordinary and very limited, of course, because of the limitations of the seeing subject. This latter theory of knowledge Gregory borrowed from Plotinus and Philo. It is to be found in all Christian thinkers after him who lean towards mysticism. There were Christian mystics before St. Gregory but he was the first who attempted a system, using the soul's reflection of the divine image as the basis of his effort.

When the Fathers gathered at Constantinople in 381 to finish what Athanasius and Basil had begun, it was to Basil's brother, Gregory, that they looked for decisive guidance. Communion with him became the test of orthodoxy in the far-reaching decisions of that council, and his was a large, if not the leading, part in inventing the technical terms which convey the doctrine of the Trinity.

A coincidence so striking in detail that it

seems no longer a coincidence is found between four cardinal scenes in Goethe's *Faust* and St Gregory's *Life of Moses*, which Goethe probably read in translation. The multiplicity of parallels here discovered argues a directness of influence on the West unique in Gregory's work.[12] That influence must be traced out, for the most part, in the works of a host of imitators.

St. Gregory of Nazianzus

The most eloquent of the " Trinity of Cappadocia" was St. Gregory of Nazianzus, called " Theologus " because of an influence in theology which rested on an erudition and expository powers which were unequalled in the fourth century and which were brought to the service of the Fourth-century Church at a crisis determinative of the future. School-fellow of Basil at Athens and co-worker, sometimes unwilling co-worker, of his maturity, Gregory was fitted by temperament for that communion with God and fellowship with books which the monastery affords ideally and did so afford himself and Basil for a few years in early manhood. And yet most of his life he had to spend in the world, disturbed by the threat of unsought distinctions and by the occasional actuality of some new, distressing eminence, forced on him by more positive spirits.

He fled back to his monastery soon after leaving it, in protest against his ordination to the priesthood, given him despite his scruples by his father, the Bishop of Nazianzus. After a few weeks' reflection he returned to Nazianzus and wrote the first of his works to give him posthumous influence, his *Apology for His Flight*. In reality it is a treatise on the priesthood, a source for a long and important series of works dealing with that office, among which St. Chrysostom's *De Sacerdotio* and Pope Gregory the Great's *Regula Pastoralis*[13] are perhaps the best known examples. It is also a source, in some of its chapters, of Bossuet's *St. Paul*.

Gregory is a poet even in his prose works and much of his declining life was given to the writing of formal poetry. He was a master of ancient prosody and has been likened to Dante for the ease and grace with which he cast the deepest thoughts of theology in poetic form. Some of his poems were much read and imitated in the East for their epigrammatic expression of ethical truths. One group of his epigrams forms the eighth book of the Greek Anthology of Constantinus Cephalus. His epigrams were translated into English in the sixteenth century; his epitaphs in the nineteenth. Other of his poems were paraphrased by Cardinal Newman,[14] to the enrichment of English verse. The following morning prayer couches the thought of Gregory in the grace that is Newman, and may be taken as typical:

> I *rise, and raise my clasped hands to Thee.*
> *Henceforth the darkness hath no part in me,*
>   *Thy sacrifice this day;*
> *Abiding firm, and with a freeman's might*
> *Stemming the waves of passion in the fight.*
>   *Ah! should I from Thee stray,*
> *My hoary head, Thy table where I bow,*
> *Will be my shame, which are mine honour now.*
> *Thus I set out; — Lord, lead me on my way! —*

As a poet, however, Gregory has been of scarcely perceptible influence in the West. His auto-biographical poems may have had a part in the formation of St. Augustine's *Confessions*, and two of his shorter poems, composed in accentual verse, may have urged on the general transference to that poetic manner.

GREEK FATHERS

When Basil died in 379, Gregory delivered a eulogy of his friend whose concluding words meet us again in Bossuet's classic *Oraison funèbre du prince de Condé*. Within a few months he was called, much against his will, to the leadership of the orthodox party in Arianized Constantinople. It was the occasion of a series of superb orations on the doctrine of the Trinity, which drew St. Jerome from his retreat in Syria. For St. Jerome, Gregory became a second master in exegesis. To this period belong the immortal *Five Theological Orations* which became the model in lucid exposition of all subsequent theologians on the Trinity and which were quoted extensively in a work joined so intimately to the medieval West as was St. John Damascene's *De Orthodoxa Fide*.

After a life of shrinking from polemical leadership, Gregory carried on in the spirit of the departed Basil for two stormy and decisive years, to the final triumph of Trinitarian orthodoxy and to one more among his many claims to direct influence on the West.

THE GREEK FATHERS

St. John Chrysostom

The Arian storms were over in the Orient when St. Chrysostom was ordained a priest and the next great heresies were to arise in the East, only when he was declining into the grave. Opportunity, if not taste and talent, denied him a place among the architects of dogma, and yet dogma is not the least of the channels whereby the most eloquent of the Greek Fathers influenced the West.

Born in Antioch of Syria and trained there in rhetoric by the great Libanius, Chrysostom like Basil and the Gregories aspired to the ascetic life. After four years in the Syrian mountains he was compelled by sickness to return to Antioch. He became a priest in 386 and gained an enormous reputation for eloquence during the next twelve years. He was consecrated Bishop of Constantinople in 398 and immediately embarked on reforms that drew the wrath of clergy and court and ultimately secured his banishment. Recalled very soon because of dismay over an earthquake that had shaken Constantinople, he was almost as promptly banished again for his protests against the noisy feasts that accompanied the raising of the empress' statue. He never returned from this second exile, dying in 407.

Within a century of his death the Orient was calling him Chrysostom, the "golden-mouthed," in tribute to the talent by which he is always first remembered. He is not only the mightiest orator of Greek Christianity; Demosthenes alone of orators who spoke in Greek has had a wider posthumous audience. His thought and pictures and very words were the texture for countless sermons in the centuries following his own. His structureless homiletic method and gorgeous rhetorical ornaments fell out of fashion at last, but not his thought, for Chrysostom by preference treated of moral themes in the pulpit, which are in fashion in every age. And he treated of them so richly and forcefully and luminously and finally that the moral thought of Chrysostom is the ultimate quarry of much solid modern preaching.

In Antioch, where most of his sermons were delivered, there had been developing from about a century before his birth a flourishing catechetical school, heir to the Aristotelian and Stoic eclectics in exegesis and therefore dedicated to the literal, grammatico-historical exposition of the Holy Books in contradistinction to the allegorizing of the Neo-Platonic Alexandrians. The majority of Chrysostom's sermons, whether turned to moral exhortation or not, are exegetical homilies after the manner of his native city. He was the most successful exemplar of her method and its saviour from total eclipse by the Alexandrians, knowing how to combine depth and breadth and delicacy as did no other Antiochene, balking not even at allegory when his author pointed the way. He has thereby nourished succeeding ages in all branches of religious life.

One so eminent in exegesis could not but play a rôle in dogmatic theology, regardless of the speculative bent of his mind. Whatever be the chief reason that recommended him so promptly and so powerfully to his own and later centuries — whether his eloquence or exegesis or sanctity or his heroic last years — Chrysostom from the morrow of his death was a mighty authority in both East and West on the content of the Faith. He was first invoked in the Latin Church, though he had been Bishop of Constantinople; he was honored in Alexandria, though he had been priest of hostile Antioch. Involved in no dogmatic controversy during his life-time, contributing nothing that can be discovered to the development of a special point of dogma in his day, he was in the thick of the controversies which arose after his death, the ally desired by all protagonists in the struggle for orthodox sanction.

No single writing of Chrysostom has been so famous, so frequently translated and printed as his dialogue *De Sacerdotio*. Dependent in part on St. Gregory of Nazianzus' *Apology for His Flight*, it is together with that work the chief source of the first treatise on pastoral theology, the *Regula Pastoralis* of Pope Gregory the Great.

Of all the ecclesiastical writers of the Early Church who treat of pedagogical questions, St. Chrysostom easily has first place. His treatise *On Pride and the Education of Children* is the first handbook of Christian education. He lays down the moral and religious basis of education and regards the school as the chief ally of the church, although he insists that the family household is the first and the indispensable training-school for the child. What progress was made in education in the fourth century is associated with his name. He revealed gifts of observation which are admired by modern historians of education and much that he has to say on instruction and superintendence and rewards and punishments is of admitted pertinence today. John Cassian, whose educational leadership touched all the Western Church, was a pupil of Chrysostom at Constantinople.

Orator, exegete, essayist, educationalist, witness to and confessor of the Faith, St. John Chrysostom is the best known and best loved of the Greek Fathers. More of him has survived, he has been translated more frequently and more widely and has been published more extensively than any other Father of the Orient. Origen alone has influenced the after-world more deeply; not even Origen has influenced it so tangibly. While Chrysostom was still a simple priest he earned a notice in St. Jerome's exclusive *De Viris Illustribus*. The Antiochenes called him "Great Teacher of the Earth" and Pope Celestine repeated the title. Within a half-century of his death he was acknowledged a doctor of the Church. Pope and patriarch and council appealed regularly to his authoritative witness. From the tenth century he was, along with St. Basil and St. Gregory of Nazianzus, one of the three Hierarchs of the Greek Church. He came to be

GREEK FATHERS

considered its greatest saint, extracts from whom were read to the people on feast-days and prescribed for edification in the monasteries. In the education of Byzantine youth he had a place along side of Homer and Isocrates. To such authority he grew in the East, as East and West fell away, breaking at times even in his Greek original the indifference of that long separation, returning to the West among the first of the Greek Fathers in Renaissance-days to meet the survivals of his Latinized self.

The career of Chrysostom as a distinct influence in the Medieval West is a chapter of vicissitudes. Cited by Jerome in the *De Viris Illustribus*, no Greek Father on the brink of the Middle Ages had more brilliant promise of Western diffusion. The Pelagian heretics were apparently his first Latin translators. At any rate they enlisted his prestige in their struggle with St. Augustine, and the greatest of Latin doctors, thus brought to a knowledge of his works, appealed to his authority and introduced him to the Latin Church in glowing eulogy. His importance for the influential Cassian has been suggested. Cassiodorus, the chief medium of the ancient culture for the Medieval West, assigned part of the works of Chrysostom as a task for his collaborators. And then the political quarrels did their work and St. Chrysostom is scarcely mentioned in Western literature from the fifth to the ninth centuries. In the Carolingian epoch he again nourishes leading thinkers, Alcuin and Rhabanus Maurus and Hincmar of Rheims being influenced by him. As the Renaissance slowly awakens into life, the rôle of Chrysostom grows. He is found in many passages of Albertus Magnus. St. Thomas Aquinas, the prince of scholastics and the central point of all subsequent Catholic theology, is deeply in debt to him and the only less important St. Bonaventure cites him frequently.

With the coming of the High Renaissance and the more extended search for authors in ancient manuscripts, Chrysostom's complete works became widely available in the West, for many of the greatest names in the new Humanism were enthusiastically devoted to him. And the greatest of the humanists surpasses them all in practical manifestation of his enthusiasm — no less than twenty-seven distinct works of Erasmus being devoted to Chrysostom.

The dogmatic battles of the Reformation were added to the enthusiasm of the Renaissance in Chrysostom's behalf, for all parties sought to make their own the authority of the *Doctor Eucharistiae*. Luther spoke almost in contempt of him, but the more objective and informed Melanchthon urgently recommended his study. Oecolampadius even translated him. A century after the Reformation period a large literature was still being produced in an effort to appropriate his authority. In seventeenth-century France he was the great model of the classic preachers. Every century since the High Renaissance — whether the motive has been religious, philological, dogmatico-historical, or humanistic — has translated and edited him. And thus his direct as well as indirect influence is still a living thing.

Pseudo-Dionysius the Areopagite

The style of St. Chrysostom, the "almost purely Attic style" it is sometimes called, is eulogized by so discriminating and detached a modern critic as Ulrich von Wilamowitz-Moellendorff.[15] The next outstanding influence from the East is amazingly inferior, symptomatic of the decline, intellectual and stylistic, which followed with inexplicable swiftness the days of Chrysostom and the Cappadocians. St. Cyril of Alexandria and Theodoret are the only intellectual exceptions; stylistically they, too, are typical of a regress, which not even theological controversy could call back to the old-time excellence. The new period lives off the old. *Florilegia* and *catenae*, compounded of excerpts from the older Fathers, come into enduring fashion. And then suddenly, so far as records tell us, there steps out of the universal mediocrity one of the strongest and certainly the strangest influence given by the East to the West.

We do not know his birth-place. We do not know his name. We are not certain even of the century in which he flourished. We only know that drawing heavily on the writings of the Neo-Platonic philosopher Proclus, he composed his works, trying to rescue from the wreck of dying paganism materials which he thought valuable to Christianity, attempting in effect a harmonization of Christianity and Platonism, and of mystical and dogmatic theology. Wishing to assure to his efforts, so it seems, the widest possible currency, he appropriated for their authorship the one name in the New Testament which most clearly suggested their purpose — something which the conventions of the time allowed. He succeeded in a way which he could not have foreseen. Probably he wrote in the fifth century and probably too in Syria. At the beginning of the sixth century, at any rate, citations from his works began to appear, and as "St. Dionysius the Areopagite," disciple of St. Paul and first Bishop of Athens, he was frequently enlisted by heretics in proof of their orthodoxy. Gradually he won authority among unquestioned Christians and by the middle of the seventh century was a widely-used orthodox weapon against heretics. In a short time he came to be regarded in the East as a kind of *Summa Theologica,* worthy of a thousand commentators. And this was only the beginning of his great and eccentric career.

In the West, Pope Gregory the Great mentioned his writings around the year 600. Pope Paul I sent copies of several of them to Pepin I, and Pope Adrian I quoted from them in a letter to Charlemagne. In 827 the Emperor Michael the Stammerer sent a copy of them to Louis the Pious, and Hilduin, Abbott of St. Denis, had them translated into Latin. Through Hilduin's activity it became widely believed that the Areopagite and the martyr Dionysius, the first Bishop of Paris and national saint of France, were identical. Another and better translation was made by John Scotus Eriügena about 858; another by John Saracenus in the twelfth century; still another by Robert Grosseteste in the thirteenth. The writings thus made available, under the name of the disciple of St. Paul, became for scholasticism a model and a source. Hugh of St. Victor, Peter Lombard, Alexander of Hales, Albert the Great, St. Bonaventure, Robert Grosseteste, Vincent of Beauvais — cardinal names in medieval scholasticism and scholarship — drew from them heavily. Dante is only the foremost of poets in debt to them.

> " Desire,
> In *Dionysius, so intensely wrought,*
> *That he, as I have done, ranged them; and named*
> *Their orders, marshal'd in his thought. From him,*
> *Dissentient, one refused his sacred read.*
> *But soon as in this heaven his doubting eyes*
> *Were open'd, Gregory at his error smiled.*
> *Now marvel, that a denizen of earth*
> *Should scan such secret truth; for he had learnt*

GREEK FATHERS

*Both this and much beside of these our orbs,
From an eye-witness to heaven's mysteries."* [16]

Shakespeare, Spenser, and Milton, perhaps unconsciously, diffused his doctrines. As Bishop Westcott [17] testifies, " His speculations on the host of heaven would have a charm for the loftiest imagination. . . . More especially was this effect increased by the blending in men's minds of his theory of the angelic orders with the once commonly accepted one of the concentric spheres. Starting, as Pococke thinks, from the Sabaeans, caught up by Plato, and from him transmitted through Philo and Macrobius and a long line of others, the belief prevailed that the heavenly orbs were the seat of intelligences, easily identified with the angelic orders of Dionysius. And thus a correspondence was established between the revolving spheres of medieval astronomy and the nine-fold hosts,

*' Who in broad circle, lovelier than the rainbow,
Girdle this round earth in a dizzy motion.'*

Spenser, when he connected the ' mighty shining christall wall,' in his *Hymne of Heavenly Beautie*, with the angels who

THE GREEK FATHERS

*'in their trinall triplicities
About Him wait, and on His will depend,'*

bears witness to the same blending of ideas; as did that still greater poet, when, in what Hallam considers 'the most sublime passage, perhaps, in Shakespeare,' he described the orbs of heaven

'Still quiring to the young-eyed cherubims.'

But the name of Milton may suffice as one last example, patent to all, of the enduring influence of the angelic conceptions of Dionysius . . . there can be no doubt that the thoughts of Dionysius have been brought home to myriads who never heard his name, through him who wrote of

'Thrones, Dominations, Princedoms, Virtues, Powers.'"

Through them alone Neo-Platonism had a place along side of Aristotelianism in Scholastic Theology; with the writings of Augustine they share honors as the literary source of later mysticism. Their most remarkable rôle was in the writings of St. Thomas Aquinas — greatest of scholastics and so potent a force in the

GREEK FATHERS

world of thought today. So much of Pseudo-Dionysius is to be found in St. Thomas' works that Abbé Darboy, who translated the Areopagite into French in 1845 and was afterwards Archbishop of Paris, declared that if the works of the Areopagite were lost, they could be reconstructed again from citations in the Angelic Doctor. In St. Thomas' hands, however, the Areopagite was servant rather than master. He cites from him continuously, but always uses him critically and is fundamentally apart from the pan-theistic tendencies so obvious in the Pseudo-Dionysian writings. In the sixteenth century Laurentius Valla cast doubt on the authenticity of the writings and inaugurated a dispute which divided the scientific world and produced a storm of controversy which did not subside until the opening of the present century.

Dionysius the Areopagite is "Pseudo-Dionysius" now to all the world of scholarship. The device whereby he gained the greatest currency for his works has been discovered and accounted for creditably to him, but his influence in theology, poetry, mystical piety remains a fact, one of the strangest facts in the history of thought and of literature. He had unusual talent as a compounder and harmonizer, but he was far happier as a philosopher than as a theologian. His most enthusiastic admirers knew how to control his aberrations and exaggerations and thus made him a constructive force in the world. No Greek Father reached the West through channels more distinguished.

St. John of Damascus

Five centuries of restless curiosity had left such a deposit of literature that the bulk, if not the complexities, of the Greek Fathers threatened the fullness of their heritage to the future. In the first three of these five centuries they had explored the last reaches of originality in their effort to rationalize the Faith. They had thereby limited their successors — save for a question or two already settled in the West — to excerpts from and summaries of their achievement or to harmonizations in the Areopagite's manner. Two centuries of excerpting had thus proceeded before the adequate summary appeared and assured to the fame of the Greek Fathers the survival of what is best in their works.

Born in Saracen Damascus in the last quarter

of the seventh century, John enjoyed a tolerance from infidel neighbors that he was not to find, later, among heretic ones. His father, an outstanding Christian, had held high office under the Caliphs, and John himself became Chief Councillor of his Mohammedan birthplace after his father's death. He later withdrew to a monastery to prepare for the priesthood and for the persecuted orthodox leadership which the Iconoclastic heresy was to give him. In this he was facing new problems and with a success that gets him mention in the histories of theology. But it is his summary of the solutions of old problems, his assembly of the wisdom of his predecessors, that is his major influence and distinction.[18] He did his work so well — with such order and accuracy and erudition and force — that those who came after could only reproduce what he had done. St. John himself called his compilation "The Fountain of Wisdom" — in tribute, no doubt, to the eminence of his sources. The title is not inaccurate of its rôle in the following centuries. Peter Lombard is only the first of Western theologians to draw from it and St. Thomas is only the greatest. From the time of its first appearance in Latin, in 1150, it was the thesaurus of Tradition for all leading scholastics, unequal, of course, to the authoritative influence of Augustine, but indispensable, nevertheless, to the comprehensiveness which they attained.

If the tale of *Barlaam and Ioasaph* is authentically his, as tradition testifies and as scholarship has not disproved, St. John was an enormous literary influence through the popularity of the story in the West. In the later Middle Ages it was a prolific source for romancers, poets, preachers, and playwrights. The taste of later ages consigned it to popular oblivion, but the materials it had furnished became the common literary property of most European peoples. And the weight of expert opinion still favors St. John as its author.

Two centuries after the Greek Patristic had done its best work, a man arose who could transmit its riches to a rapidly estranging world. In transmitting the work of his predecessors, however imperfectly, St. John would have been a benefactor to the unhellenic West. In transmitting it so masterfully, he became a Father to all the Church in the strictest meaning of the term, the last of those who wrote in Greek to whom the term applies unchallenged.

III. THE FOURTH AND FIFTH CENTURIES

THE summary of the Greek Fathers by the last of them was essential to their later currency. Not even the Greek-speaking East could have dispensed with St. John of Damascus. The Byzantine mind, clerical and lay, was first of all theological. And Byzantine theology after St. John's time was always thoroughly traditional. It looked to the Fathers of the Golden Age for guidance in its problems. It found that guidance effective for the most part only with St. John's *Summa*. Not every Greek theologian could have kept the Fathers on his finger-tips.

The West too was to need St. John. From an early date it needed more. Greek was dying visibly in the West from the middle of the second century. Latin translations of cherished Greek Fathers began to appear soon after, language being only the earliest foretaste of the separation of the East and the West. Differences in character, mutually irritating, which had ante-dated the Empire and which the Empire could not efface and the Church could only soften; differences in tongue and ways of thought patent even amid the cosmopolitanism of the Empire's first two centuries; memories of the ancient antagonisms which had preceded the *Pax Romana* — all awoke to life again as the *Pax Romana* faded. The founding of Constantinople as a second Rome precipitated the inevitable division, though the Arian controversy arrested its progress so far as the Church was concerned. Western churchmen even studied in the East during the widest stress of Arianism, affording to the Fathers of the Golden Age a few direct Western contacts. These contacts grew always fewer, however, as the menace of Arianism weakened and finally, even in their Latin dress, the Greek Fathers were a rarity. The halves of the Empire were rejoined for a space before the collapse of the West in the sixth century. The exchanges of commerce were still a bond at the beginning of the eighth; oneness of faith survived quarrel and schism well into the eleventh, and then even the halves of the Church fell apart in a divorce that still endures. Early in the fifth century, however, the Greek Fathers felt the division,

THE IVTH AND VTH CENTURIES

and their lessened rôle in the Western world stretches through a thousand years.

In the century preceding this long eclipse they were a tangible power in the West. The hegemony in thought which they had always enjoyed, despite growing Western indifference, attained to a new effectiveness then under the goad of aggressive heresy. The second half of the third century had been fruitful in Latin translations, that cherished works of the older Fathers might survive the decay of Greek. The second half of the fourth century began such another period when St. Hilary of Poitiers returned from the East, a disciple of the Greek Patristic. Arianism was but one of the many problems which were facing the Latin doctors, but it served to recall to their groping minds the diversity of Greek preeminence. To questions strange to the Hellenic East they might not find in the East an answer, but principles and methods they were bound to find there suited, as of old, to their purpose. In the Latin West, as in the Greek East, this was the Golden Age and its larger minds, beyond the moment's needs, explored the Greek achievement.

Our knowledge of the Latin translations of the time is still very fragmentary,[19] but among its fragments names stand out that stand out first with us. The age agrees with the twentieth century on its hierarchy of excellence for the Greek Fathers. Origen was being put into Latin; Hilary, Rufinus, and Jerome each taking a hand in the work. The exegetical writings and the *De Principiis*, in versions more and less faithful, began to nourish Latin minds whom the originals could not reach and to stir up quarrels, dogmatic and other, which divided even Origen's admirers. Eusebius' *On Easter* and *Life of Constantine* were latinized early in the fourth century and his *Ecclesiastical History*, through Rufinus' offices, at the beginning of the fifth. His *Chronicle*, as revised and augmented by Jerome and in Jerome's Latin version, has always been one of the fundamental assumptions of Western historical research. Parts of St. Basil and St. Gregory of Nazianzus, St. Athanasius' *Life of St. Anthony*, large sections of St. Chrysostom, the treatises of lesser Fathers, epistles and gospels, martyrdoms and acts, all joined by way of translation at this time the literary acquisitions of the West.

The outstanding figures in the fourth century West are Hilary and Ambrose and Jerome.

THE IVTH AND VTH CENTURIES

All three of them knew Greek well and the works of Greek Fathers intimately. Hilary, if Tertullian be excluded, is the first great Latin theologian, as in effectiveness he is one of the first. By him Arianism in Gaul and Italy is crushed at the height of its progress — with the ideas of Athanasius, however, working through a Western mind. If the times could boast of Roman temperaments, St. Ambrose is one of these, and yet his works reflect the Greek Fathers almost to the exclusion of the Latin. Origen and Athanasius and Cyril of Jerusalem appear again in his pages. In 380, Gregory of Nazianzus delivered his *Theological Orations*. In 381 they reached the West through Ambrose's *De Spiritu Sancto*. So closely did he follow St. Basil's *Hexaemeron* in his own work of that name that the very phrasing of Basil's thought accompanies that thought into Latin, and he is equally faithful in following Basil in a number of minor works. St. Jerome could coin an epigram in derision of Ambrose's borrowings, yet his own comprehensive scholarship included a Greek Father even to errors.[20] Under the personal inspiration of Nazianzus for a period during the latter's Constantinople days, disciple of Origen's exegesis throughout his laborious youth, deeply in debt to Eusebius's work to the point of occasional appropriation, Jerome, like Hilary and Ambrose, was largely inspired by the Greeks. He wove into the woof of his own originality a considerable Greek Christian inheritance. He gave to that inheritance, beyond its current translations, a place in Western tradition.

Of the Latin Fathers of the fifth century John Cassian certainly knew Greek and carried into his mighty influence on Western monasticism the effects of Greek discipleship. He gives way, as do all his contemporaries, however, in any survey of the fifth century, before the towering personality of St. Augustine.

If St. Augustine had known no Greek [21] or no Greek Father, he would still be a large consideration in this essay, for his career conditioned the future of the remotest thought of his time. In the intellectual formation of one, to whose influence in the history of Western ideas only Plato's and Aristotle's compare, whose domination of medieval philosophy and theology suggests the exclusiveness of a monopoly and who yet can be hailed by contemporary philosophers as the "first modern man" — in

THE IVTH AND VTH CENTURIES

the mental make-up of this colossus, what is the share of the Greek Fathers?

If he were only their Western mouthpiece, more effective than all others such because of an arresting style and an expounding instinct superlatively adapted to the West, then the Greek Fathers were the major force in medieval and modern Christianity, hidden beneath the phrases of an African rhetorician. St. Augustine was not thus eminent as an expounder, however eminent as a stylist; he was only the mouthpiece of his own endowments as enriched by the heritage of his day.

If we glance through the pages of Augustine's works, the names of Greek Fathers meet us — Irenaeus and Origen and Basil and Nazianzus and Chrysostom and others. If we look more closely here and there, we find Greek doctrine quoted and appropriated. We know that he read Eusebius' *Chronica* to the benefit of his *City of God*.[22] We are certain that Origen and Basil were addressing him, through Ambrose's lips and language, from Ambrose's pulpit in those wavering days before he gave himself to God. He demanded a Latin version of the Greek commentators for his own scriptural exegesis and in his *De Trinitate* he more

THE GREEK FATHERS

than once shows preference for Greek opinions. Augustine, in short, as any man, bore the impress of his times, and in the Christian world of his catechumenate years the Greek Fathers still were sovereign. That sovereignty in the West was to fade forever before his creative originality, but only after Augustine too had been nourished on its traditions. For over two hundred years that sovereignty had prevailed despite accumulating causes for its overthrow, until the genius of Augustine joined with migrations from the North to break the Greek ascendancy. A century after Augustine's death in 430 the Greek Fathers were all but forgotten in the scenes of their long hegemony. They came to the Western Middle Ages, but chiefly in the Western tradition, hidden for the most part in the works of men who had drawn from Augustine and other disciples.

IV. FROM THE FIFTH THROUGH THE FIFTEENTH CENTURY

FOR a thousand years after Augustine's time the Greek Fathers were eclipsed in the West. They had influenced the earlier Latin Fathers too largely and too long not to be still an influence on later generations. But it was an anonymous influence for the most part, an element unrecognized in an accepted common tradition. Of direct contacts through translations instances occur, but notable alike in Western thought for their importance and their rarity. From the far end of the Mediterranean, Byzantium towers over Europe, recalling to the once imperial West the grandeur which the West had lost. The Greek Fathers are honored in Byzantium and are the center of intellectual life, and something of their intellectual primacy finds lodgement in the West — a vague conception of lofty eminence such as mythical heroes enjoy, mistaken in scattered Western places for the Byzantine reality. Twice in these long centuries the reality breaks through and stirs up Western lethargy into what finally becomes a revival. The continuity of history cannot date these revivals precisely, but it is well into the fifteenth century before their effects are widely felt and the Greek Fathers as a group emerge from their long eclipse.

The Latin West knew little Greek for most of this thousand years. In Gaul there still were Greek Colonies in the sixth and seventh centuries. In Ireland a knowledge of the language persisted well into the ninth. Irish scholars were the Greek scholars in Charlemagne's Latin revival. England harbored a restricted Hellenism for something less than a century after a Greek monk of Tarsus was raised to the see of Canterbury. In Italy the knowledge of Greek was never wholly extinguished. In South Italy and Sicily it remained a living tongue and Basilian monasteries which sprung up there were centers of Hellenic culture. Papal hospitality during the Iconoclast controversy drew many Greeks to Italy. In Naples throughout the Middle Ages Greek was a written language. But these are either short-lived instances or local, if in fact persistent. Even Italy as a whole was insensible of its Greek-speaking colonies. Movements which in later times would have rung throughout the West were subject then to that excessive localism which the Northern migrations had brought. Roger Bacon in the thirteenth century, for all his intelligence and effort, could achieve only the rudiments in a life-time's pursuit of Greek. Petrarch in the fourteenth century, even with a Greek-speaking tutor, could not read Homer and Plato, so scarce and unavailable were the keys to the written language. A few years after Petrarch's death these keys began to multiply, to unlock, however, only pagan treasures to Renaissance enthusiasm. The Greek Fathers were a second love even for Christian humanists and they followed in the wake of pagan classics by an interval of about a century. Whatever new influence the Greek Fathers enjoy during their thousand years' eclipse must be mostly through Latin translations that somehow arise in the West.

The sixth century produced many such under the enlightened stimulus of Cassiodorus. In his striving to make erudition a feature of monastic life, he induced a certain Mutianus to translate the *Homilies* of St. Chrysostom on the *Epistle to the Hebrews*. To his impulse are traced Latin versions of parts of Gregory

THE GREEK FATHERS

of Nyssa, of Clement of Alexandria, of Origen; of the church-histories of Socrates of Constantinople, Sozomen, and Theodoret and many other works canonical, exegetical, and dogmatic. And yet their subject-matter would scarcely have appealed beyond the circles of the learned. The pagan classics were being studied again under the impulse of the same Cassiodorus. He even wrote a manual of profane studies which the Middle Ages treasured. We have long lists of medieval writers bearing traces of such studies.[23] No list nor catalogue nor school program can show like abundance for the Greek Fathers. The Christian authors generally, some Christian poets excepted, were reserved to liturgical offices and to the meditations of educated clerics. Boethius, Cassiodorus, Gregory the Great, Isidore of Seville are the outstanding savants of the sixth and seventh centuries. Only Boethius among them certainly knew Greek and only Gregory was a channel for a Greek Father. And these are the scholars and organizers, along with Martianus Capella, who in serving their own times were the teachers for the Middle Ages.

The earliest foretaste of a better fortune came in the ninth century with the literary and artistic revival which Charlemagne inaugurated. It was essentially a Latin revival which went out from Charlemagne's circle. Its leading men either knew no Greek or knowing it could not use it widely, in the great dearth of Greek texts at the time. About the middle of the century, however, when Charlemagne long was dead and his Renaissance and monarchy were dying, a Greek author was turned into Latin who became a master-influence on following generations. John Scotus Eriügena learned his Greek in Ireland before Scandinavian depredations there drove him to the continent, but not even an idealized Irish Hellenism accounts for his achievement — how in a century most unhellenic, on the French side of the Pyrenees, he translated Greek authors acceptably and, of all Greek authors extant in the world, the vague and involved Areopagite! The translation inaugurated by the Abbot Hilduin, earlier in the century, had been found unsatisfactory, apparently. John succeeded with a success that on its linguistic side evoked the astonishment of Anastasius, the Greek librarian of the Pope. The immediate fruit of his Latin version was its effect upon himself, the most considerable Western thinker between St. Augustine and St. Anselm. Gregory of Nyssa, whom he translated in part, and Gregory of Nazianzus had also share in his formation, but the Areopagite was the permanent influence of his mature intellectual life. The translation was felt to be an important event even during John's own lifetime — important enough to engage the attention of Anastasius in a painstaking revision — but neither translation nor original enjoyed a vogue just then. Later they both bulk large in the intellectual life of the West; in the ninth century they were but precursors, the one of the rising scholasticism, the other of the renaissance of the Greek Fathers.[24]

The tenth century was a fallow time for letters and learning generally, though it could boast of monasteries like St. Gall and Corbie and of Hroswitha, the nun of Gandersheim. Of Greek scholarship in the period very little can be said. The eleventh century began a brighter season and at Monte Cassino, for practical ends, even Greek works were translated. Thus the *Regulae* of St. Basil, some sermons of Gregory Nazianzen, a treatise each of Origen and Chrysostom found their way into Latin — isolated phenomena, so far as scholarship can tell, at the mercy of the localism which weighed down upon the West.

The Ninth-century Renaissance had been an almost wholly Latin revival, which had faded away to decadence, outside monastic walls, in the civil wars of Charlemagne's successors. With the twelfth century came another renaissance, much wider in its interests, more permanent in results, and in it Greek had part as well as Latin. It was an expansive, vigorous age in which the first Crusades were fought and Roman Law returned to Western science. Amid the development of Gothic architecture and of the nascent university, the rise of towns and growth of native literatures, it accepted the Latin classics, particularly the Latin poets, but for Greek it was practical in its preferences. Greek mathematics and medicine, Greek philosophy and theology intrigued it to the exclusion of other phases. Beyond the Italian Alps it was dubious of its Greek, where it was not indifferent to it, and seemed to value the most painfully literal translator. South of the Italian Alps, in Italy and Sicily, Greek was very frequently a vernacular. The Crusades, which did so much to seal the old estrangements, did nothing of themselves for the spread of Greek.

THE GREEK FATHERS

But trade arose in Northern Europe and quickened in the South in the common purpose found against the Moslem. Merchants followed promptly the paths of the Crusaders, and East and West once more were joined in commerce. A Pisan and Venetian quarter grew up at Constantinople where a number of Western scholars learned Greek. A constant stream of embassies, particularly from Rome and Pisa and Gaul, gave further impulse to the resurrection of Western Hellenism. And from Spain and the Near East came the hellenized Arabic learning which the new reaches of commerce were disseminating. Of the various sources of Hellenism in the Twelfth-century Renaissance, the indirect, Arabic source was most prolific. And the contacts thus afforded weakened the ancient localism, and translations came in response to new demands.

What was now the Norman kingdom of Sicily and South Italy had never lost all contact with the East. Its chief cities had formed part of ancient Magna Graecia, and, as Greek towns, long persisted under Rome. Later and for centuries and during the thinnest times of commerce, Byzantium held them in nominal sovereignty. And now under Norman masters, amid Latin and Arabic elements, they still had a Greek-speaking population. Thanks to Basilian monks who had found asylum there, large Greek libraries were assembled in its monasteries. The nearest of civilized European states to the Greek and Arabic East and near the Eastern trade-lanes of Spain and farther Europe, it concentrated in itself the advantages scattered elsewhere, reinforced by the strength of its traditions. In this tri-lingual kingdom, translations must have come even without the rising tide of a revival. Here under William I, among many similar enterprises, a Latin version of Nazianzus was begun.

North of the Norman kingdom, in the expanding commercial cities, some Latins knew Greek from trading contacts. The three men most skilled in the two languages, outside the Norman kingdom, were James of Venice, Moses of Bergamo, and Burgundio of Pisa. Burgundio, whose zeal for translating extended to pagan authors, was interested in Greek theology before all other phases of Hellenism and was thereby immensely influential on Latin thought. He translated some homilies of Chrysostom, St. Basil on *Isaiah,* and above all, part of the *De Orthodoxa Fide* of St. John of Damascus.

THE GREEK FATHERS

St. John owes his important rôle in Latin thought primarily to Burgundio's work. It was his translation that was used by such cardinal architects of Latin thought as Peter Lombard and St. Thomas Aquinas. North of the Alps the advantages which Italy enjoyed were almost unknown and the record of Greek translations correspondingly feeble. Some of St. John of Damascus was translated in Germany and Hungary. In France, John Saracenus translated Pseudo-Dionysius — a crude performance but important, because of its use by John of Salisbury, then, and its later service to Albert the Great and St. Thomas Aquinas.

What was done for the Greek Fathers in the twelfth-century revival was a constructive, permanent work in Western thought, but neither Greek nor the Greek Fathers were known to the most of what was then educated Europe.

During the thirteenth century the general scantiness of Greek learning continued, although the monasteries south of the Alps were stored with Greek manuscripts and the old contacts with the East were sustained and increased by trade. This was the age of Dante who knew not Greek and of St. Thomas who may have known some,[25] who in any case used St. Chrysostom and other Greek Fathers and was deeply in debt to the Areopagite. By two of St. Thomas' contemporaries, even beyond the Alps, the Greek Fathers were felt to be important; Roger Bacon, the Franciscan monk, and Robert Grosseteste, the Bishop of Lincoln. We feel certain that Bacon, though the author of a Greek grammar heroically compiled and one of the first minds of his time, could never read connected Greek prose, and that Grosseteste somehow could. One of Bacon's dismal pictures of thirteenth century Hellenism makes express exception for "my Lord Robert, Bishop of Lincoln."

"Numberless portions of the wisdom of God are wanting to us. Many books of the sacred text remain untranslated. . . . Numberless books again of Hebrew and Greek expositors are wanting to the Latins. . . . The Church therefore is slumbering. She does nothing in this matter, nor hath done these seventy years; save that my Lord Robert, Bishop of Lincoln, of holy memory, did give to the Latins some part of the writings of St. Dionysius and of Damascene, and some other holy Doctors."[26] It was a remarkable feat, even in conjunction

THE GREEK FATHERS

with a Greek-speaking coadjutor, to have translated Greek prose in Grosseteste's England, where not even the library at Canterbury retained a trace of Archbishop Theodore. Grosseteste is more remarkable for the subjects which he chose. He not only undertook a new version of the Areopagite and did something for the *De Orthodoxa Fide* of St. John of Damascus, but he reached back beyond the beginnings of Christian Hellenism to Primitive Christianity and gave the *Epistles* of St. Ignatius to the Latin West. For his own time and for the whole Middle Ages he was eccentric in this; only a much later age was to emulate his interest in Christian origins.

Whenever the Renaissance began, the Renaissance with the large R, which used to be dated from the Fall of Constantinople in 1453, no one doubts that it began to flower in the fourteenth century with Petrarch and Boccaccio. It was a pagan flowering for the most part and decidedly more Latin than Greek. Only towards the close of the century did Chrysoloras arrive in Florence and only in the next century did Greek and the Greek Fathers begin to flourish. Meanwhile Petrarch and Boccaccio, like Roger Bacon before them, were propagandists in the cause of Greek, a language which they, too, never learned. Unlike Bacon their propaganda had results. They imposed on a generation primarily concerned with a revival of Latin classics the conviction that Greek belonged by right to that revival. Nothing could be done about it then in the dearth of Greek teachers and grammars and texts, but they kept to their conviction and gathered Greek manuscripts and their successors welcomed Chrysoloras with emphasis. The enthusiasm which he stirred up cooled before the difficulties of the language and the Italian preference for Latin and the Renaissance preference for Cicero, but there was an abundance of manuscripts in Italy, and perhaps fifteen or twenty Italians were competent to read them, when the Fall of Constantinople released more teachers and manuscripts to swell the rising tide.

The Greek Fathers, during the last century of their eclipse, were not cultivated even in Italy, despite the materials at hand for their revival. With the fifteenth century came a change. Basilian monasteries were no longer the chief repositories of their works. In the library of the Vatican, sections of Chrysostom,

THE GREEK FATHERS

of Cyril of Alexandria, of Eusebius and Irenaeus were found in the middle of the century — a small group in so huge a collection, but indicative of the change which was in progress. Later in the century, parts of Gregory of Nazianzus and Basil and Athanasius and much more of Chrysostom were added. Translations began to appear in great numbers, Ambagio Traversari becoming especially distinguished in such work. This rapid emergence from the scattered, if important, contacts of the previous centuries was not due to the contemporary pursuit of Greek. The Fathers were part of Greek antiquity and therefore to be cultivated. But they were also part of Christian antiquity. And it was Christian antiquity just then which was commanding much Western attention. A reform was afoot within the Church which required their testimony and example.

Leading minds of the time were weary of the barren formalism into which Scholastic Theology had fallen. It had always been enormously concerned with the logical continuity of doctrines, and in emphasizing their logical consistency it grew to minimize their scriptural source. In the ruthless application of its method, despite its reverence for the Scriptures, scriptural ideas and theological reasoning tended in time to separate. Even in its golden epoch this danger had been sensed. Meanwhile Scholasticism had fallen. It had not kept pace with the sciences; it had forgotten one of the aspirations of the soul. It had failed to remember that contemplation as well as demonstration is an abiding human need. It had wasted its strength for a hundred years on trifles from a greater age. It was become an empty dialectic, a perpetual parade of logical ingenuity and of terminology fantastically elaborate. At a time when other sciences were swelling the content of a knowledge with which theology would have to reckon, Scholasticism stood still in self-imposed starvation.

By the middle of the fifteenth century its inadequacy was become so distressing that earnest souls rose everywhere in protest. In Germany, Cardinal Nicolaus of Cusa; in Italy, Pico della Mirandola and Ficino; in Spain, Cardinal Ximenes and his circle; in France, Lefèvre d'Étaples; in England, Pico's pupil, John Colet — men various in temperament and outlook but all determined to do what they could for the rejuvenation of Sacred Science.

THE GREEK FATHERS

The contemporary return to pagan antiquity was restoring a treasury of knowledge to the mind. A return to Christian antiquity would do as much for the spirit. So at least they thought. They broke with the immediate past, with the scholasticism of their day, and sought to renew religion in the first ages of the Church. For all of them this meant a return to the Bible in the first place; for some it meant the return to the Fathers as well. And for the Greek Fathers themselves it meant many translations and some circulation of their works before the dawn of the sixteenth century and the maturity of Erasmus.

V. HIGH RENAISSANCE AND THE REFORM OF ECCLESIASTICAL LEARNING

ONE of the remarkable facts about the High Renaissance is that it was not precisely a renaissance. It was not a re-birth of something that once had been and then had ceased to be. Neither in its spirit nor in its content was it essentially a renewal. In spirit it was unconsciously medieval, even when loudly atheistic. It followed the path of authority, though it was a dead antiquity and not a living church to which it frequently yielded the tribute of its obedience. Later on, in the seventeenth century, the rational spirit grew strong. But in the sixteenth were only the unconscious beginnings. Authority seemed to clash with authority as the century grew old, the Renaissance man was driven to make comparisons, the spirit of criticism emerged, to be a characteristic, however, only of a later time. In content the Renaissance — no matter how far back we trace it — was largely an expansion of what had always been — the ancient Latin culture. It had Greek elements also in the last two centuries of its course, but previously it had been overwhelmingly Latin, and without Greek and the Fathers, there would still have been a "High Renaissance" in the expansive sixteenth century. Throughout the Middle Ages the Latin culture had persisted, diminished by barbarian invasions, confined for the most part to monasteries, largely misinterpreted, but persistent nevertheless until its revival under Petrarch and Boccaccio. In the time of the High Renaissance, in the age of the voyages of discovery and of the discovery of typography, there was an enrichment of experience astounding in its swiftness, an enlargement of the horizons of the world and of the intellect unparalleled in its measure and suddenness. Men were bewildered and exhilarated by the wealth and variety of their present acquisitions and eager for more. The growing revival of the preceding centuries took on a new intensity, but it was still a revival, not a renaissance; an acceleration and elaboration of what Petrarch and Boccaccio had particularized, not a re-birth. In its Greek and patristic aspects the Renaissance was more nearly a renaissance. But not even the Greek Fathers, as we have seen, had been lost to the West completely during their thousand years' eclipse.

And the same must be said of the Reformation in its contacts with the Fathers. It gave impetus and acceleration to what already was; it did not originate. Its doctrines required the authority of Tradition and therefore the testimony of the Fathers. Its opponents required refutation by Tradition and therefore the testimony of the Fathers. Augustine and Jerome were the leading witnesses thus enlisted from antiquity, but the Greek Fathers too were summoned as the conflict widened and deepened. To the theological motive of the fifteenth century — the desire for patristic instructors — was now added the polemical — the desire for patristic protagonists. The reformers of the fifteenth century had sought an enrichment of the doctrines already contained in the Scholastics; the Protestants of the sixteenth century were seeking to subvert these doctrines. The polemical or apologetic motive thus became an abiding force in the West — to the vast development of dogma and a new influence for the Greek Fathers.

The greatest of humanists — if leadership be the test — was also the man who did most for the revival of the Greek Fathers. Desiderius Erasmus of Rotterdam gave to the restricted efforts of Pico and Ficino and Nicolaus of Cusa a European importance. Hostile to the Reformation as a menace to Humanism,[27] and hostile to Scholasticism in its unworthy, contemporary representatives, he typifies the sovereign confidence of his time in the efficacy of the works of antiquity. He found the nourishment for his intellectual life in the masterpieces of the ancients; he thought to find sufficient nourishment for the moral life in the records of early Christianity. If men could only come to know their Saviour and His teaching in the documents of the Early Church, they would inevitably live after Him, so compelling were His personality and doctrine, when disembarrassed of theological strata. To find Christ it was only necessary to apply the science of Philology to sacred texts as it was then being applied to profane ones. Erasmus was interested primarily in the Scriptures and hence his famous, if not too accurate, Greek

HIGH RENAISSANCE

Testament. But philological method compelled the use of related documents and hence his interest in the Fathers, in the theologians of the Early Church. After his Greek New Testament appeared, he published, besides certain of the Latin Fathers, St. Irenaeus, Origen, St. Chrysostom, and parts of St. Basil and St. Athanasius among the Greek. But it was always the Gospel which he was seeking in these early testimonies. Regardless of the Socratic error which underlay his program, of his ignorance of the inevitableness of theology, of the almost exclusively evangelical motive of his approach, he gave to the revival of the Greek Fathers the prestige of one miscalled the "Renaissance Voltaire" in tribute to his towering contemporary influence. Humanists of the day were printing editions of the Fathers merely because they too were of the magic past. The interest and example of Erasmus gave a new point and assurance to their industry.

It was in England that Erasmus found the greatest support for his efforts, where humanists did not pretend to the paganism affected by many Italians. Consciously or unconsciously Englishmen followed in the footsteps of Bacon and Grosseteste among their own countrymen and of Pico and Ficino from abroad. They were churchmen, for the most part, who were interested in a revival of letters and a reform of theological method. In England Greek had begun to spread early in the preceding century. William Selling, Prior of Canterbury, had turned a sermon of Chrysostom into Latin — the earliest recorded expression of a revival which kept expanding until the Reformation quarrels spelled its doom. John Colet in the latter fifteenth century brought the spirit of Pico and Ficino to England, expounded the *Epistles* of St. Paul in the new manner, and wrote several treatises under the obvious influence of the Areopagite. In the last years of the century he did much to confirm Erasmus in his distrust of the later Schoolmen. In 1517 Bishop Fox, the Protector of the University of Oxford, gave official and effective impetus to the views of Colet and Erasmus. He commanded the teaching of the early Fathers rather than of the scholastic doctors and compelled all students of the University to study Greek. Cambridge admitted similar legislation. A great battle followed between the " Greeks " and the " Trojans," as the protagonists and opponents of the Greek Fathers called themselves, a battle almost comic in retrospect, though it echoed beyond college walls and even cost lives in its more violent moments. Finally the King and Wolsey interfered, the ideas of Colet prevailed, and the study of the Greek Fathers enjoyed an accepted place in the University curricula. It proved a triumph of method for the most part. The Platonism of the Greek Fathers left few traces on the records of the time. The Areopagite was failing as an effective force in England. In the battles being precipitated by the oncoming Reformation even Platonists like Sir Thomas More returned to the classic arguments of the Schoolmen. On the eve of the royal aggression against the established ecclesiastical order, Greek learning seems to have been widely diffused among the upper classes, even as the study of Greek was secured in the Universities, in Colet's foundation at St. Paul's, and in the grammar schools old and new. And then both grammar schools and Greek, along with monasteries and libraries, gave way before the fury of the Reformers. If Greek and the Greek Fathers persisted as a discipline, if Ascham and Lady Jane Grey and Spenser were hellenists after a fashion, Greek learning in the large was lost in the turmoil. The long years of Elizabeth saw only a few translations, occasioned by religious controversy. All else is a blank to us for Greek studies, patristic or pagan, in the land fairest with promise for Erasmus' hopes.

And in other countries a Greek decline set in after brilliant expectations. Italian humanism was too popular in its reaches to indulge with long immunity its pagan affectations. Always more Latin than Greek, it passed under a cloud after the first decade of the century, restricted to a diminishing life in the study and schoolroom. Baronius in Church History and Bellarmine in theology are two of the glories of the time in Italy, men eminent in the polemical scholarship of their own day and still indispensable in ours, despite all the acquisitions meanwhile of Western scholarship. And yet they too exhibit the defect common to later sixteenth-century Italy — scanty acquaintance with the language of the Greek Fathers. In France, Greek was cultivated enthusiastically among the learned, taking deep root in certain minds — Stephanus, Budé, Casaubon — but touching only lightly the educated as a whole. Latin, enthroned by centuries of literary usage and by sentimental memories of the ancient empire, reinforced by the affinity between French and Roman character, remained the classic language of the nation. In Geneva the French Calvin was at first vastly interested in the Primitive Church as a pattern for his own and therefore in the witness of early Greek Fathers. But Greek, for all the intensity of its earlier cultivation, could not withstand the Wars of Religion. The consuming curiosity of a man like Montaigne never took him far into Greek. The manners of the time permitted almost verbatim appropriation of ancient authors into one's own work and, in this, Montaigne was emphatically in fashion. St. Augustine and Lactantius, among the Latin Fathers, are easily uncovered in his pages, there being forty-two undoubted borrowings from the *City of God* alone. A most exacting scrutiny for the Greek Fathers yields only a few dubious passages from Eusebius.[28] And Montaigne in the seclusion of his tower was the one French man-of-letters who could have perused the Greek Fathers at leisure, had his tastes so dictated, undisturbed by the turmoil about him.

Germany, which in a later time was to lead

THE GREEK FATHERS

all Europe in understanding of ancient culture, lagged behind other countries then, despite the abundance of its erudition. Some of her humanists were theologians and therefore directly concerned with the Greek Fathers and many of her humanists included the Greek Fathers in their labors out of deference to Erasmus' interest. Luther — in no sense a humanist — advocated the study of the Fathers [29] and necessarily did much to promote their study, particularly in his early Protestant years. For a time Pseudo-Dionysius was his mystic guide.[30] In controversy with Zwingli he appealed to Fathers both Greek and Latin.[31] He encouraged the editing of certain works of Athanasius. He was never himself affected deeply and directly by the Greek Fathers and formally withdrew his approval of them, as his fundamental opposition to Erasmus grew clearer. In his later years he was even abusive of Chrysostom.[32] Melanchthon, on the other hand, was too much the humanist, too thoroughly penetrated by Erasmus, to follow Luther here. It was Melanchthon, in fact, who reduced the ideas of Erasmus to a system. His systematization came too late, however, like much else in Melanchthon's life; under the eloquence of

HIGH RENAISSANCE

Luther the younger theologians were turning elsewhere, but something of the tradition of Erasmus went with them, at least something of that taste for Christian Antiquity and the Greek Fathers, imposed by the prestige of Erasmus and by the authority of that Philip Melanchthon who was at once the founder of Evangelical theology and the *Praeceptor Germaniae*. Among some other leaders of the Reformation this tradition was strong; in Oecolampadius, for instance, who translated part of Gregory of Nazianzus, and in the Swiss Zwingli, who was read in Origen and Chrysostom as well as Augustine and particularly attached to the christological expositions of the Greek Fathers. It was a personal acquisition, for the most part, however, and not to be bequeathed in large measure to successors. Calvinism became a mighty force in Protestantism as the century grew old, a kind of Protestantism become scholastic, that wiped out all tradition between the Gospel and itself and therefore levelled the Greek Fathers in its progress. The Fathers survived as a vital force, nevertheless, even among Protestants as new needs kept demanding patristic testimony; as Catholic theology, under the leadership of Melchior Cano, turned more and more to their perusal. But interest in them was not tangibly on the increase at the close of a century that at its opening promised much and achieved much for their influence.

VI. THE SEVENTEENTH AND EIGHTEENTH CENTURIES

WHAT the enthusiasm of the sixteenth century could not achieve in reviving the study of Greek, the seventeenth did not even attempt. In the educational theory of the High Renaissance Greek had been prized as highly as Latin. Erasmus had declared that the two languages should be taught together. Programs of study had recommended long lists of Greek authors, Christian as well as pagan. But Greek under the most favorable conditions had gained only half the class-hours devoted to Latin and only selections from Greek Fathers such as Chrysostom had won scanty place in curricula. The West was Latin, not Greek, in culture — a fact against which even the authority of Erasmus had not prevailed. And Erasmus now was dead and Descartes was in the ascendant — Descartes and France. The study of Greek, according to Descartes, was of as little value as the study of the " Jargon of Bretony."[33]

And his age lived up largely to his dictum. Cartesianism developed the "ego" so emphatically and campaigned for originality so violently that many contemporary writers treated antiquity with condescension at the very time they were being nourished on its treasures. There was a memorable battle in the century known to the History of Literature as "Le Querelle des Anciens et des Moderns." It was precipitated by the rejection of Aristotle from authority in philosophy and the enthronement of reason by Descartes. It resolved into a quarrel over method, however, rather than of ultimate objective. Even the "Ancients" did not approve the servile antiquarianism of the Renaissance. They too had in view the emancipation of the French genius. They wished only not to lose what was appropriate in antiquity to that genius' flowering. The actual achievements of France at the time encouraged them in their efforts — efforts which did not make for precision or diffusion of Greek knowledge. To the exacting twentieth century it is a mystery how so many authors of the day could approximate the ancient Greeks in subject-matter, view-point, and success, and yet know Greek originals mostly through shabby

XVIITH AND XVIIITH CENTURIES

translations. There were accomplished hellenists in the century, but they were rare among classical writers. And we have the testimony of the most accomplished hellenist of them all, Fénelon, that all these preparatory studies (Greek included) "have more appearance than solidity."[34] In the decadence of her Greek, as in the preeminence of her thought, France was the pattern for Europe.

The *Ratio Studiorum* of the Jesuits called for St. Gregory of Nazianzus, St. Basil, and St. Chrysostom among Greek authors to be studied, but the teaching of neither Greek nor the Greek Fathers was accompanied by wide success among these, the most influential and effective teachers of the day. The unrivalled expounders of Greek at the time were the community of Port-Royal, the preceptors of so many of the age's greatest men. But the contacts of Port-Royal were too few, however important in other respects, to constitute or threaten an exception to Fénelon's statement. Greek in that day was taught chiefly as an honor's course. A precise knowledge of it was thought to be valuable in medicine or theology. In the latter field superb work was done, some of which is literature as well as science, some of which is more literature than science, and on either count the Greek Fathers play a rôle.

The humanists of the sixteenth century had been prodigal in printing Greek Fathers. Early in the seventeenth century and largely under the initiative of the Jesuits, the production of patristic works became a phase of the Counter-Reformation. Excellent editions of Christian writers began to issue from the Paris presses, some of which after three hundred years are prized by scholars. Thus Fronton de Duc edited a famous edition of Chrysostom. Andreas Schott, Sirmond, and Denis Petau won immortal names in Greek patristic scholarship. This was the age when the enormous enterprise of the Bollandists, still unfolding in our time, was inaugurated, and the great patristic work of the Benedictines of St. Maur was organized. Theological controversy became less reasoning, less scriptural, more patristic, more historical, following the impulse of the Centuriators and Baronius. It was a polemical historiography which thus reached back for weapons to the Church's early age and uncovered a mighty arsenal of learning. But regardless of its motives, it promoted the serious study of the Fathers in a time fallow for Hellenism generally.

XVIITH AND XVIIITH CENTURIES

At the turn of the century St. Francis de Sales was in the heyday of his momentous, many-sided career. Superbly educated; a humanist; a hellenist who knew Aristotle, Plato, and Epictetus; a French man-of-letters who was one of the major factors in the formation of literary French, St. Francis was deeply read in the Greek Fathers and reflects them freely in some of his most influential works. To his "Treatise on the Love of God," the fecund source of a veritable library of practical piety effective in our day, St. Gregory of Nazianzus, St. John Chrysostom, and Pseudo-Dionysius the Areopagite are frequent and acknowledged contributors.

Of all the phases of French literature in a period made illustrious by at least twelve immortal writers, none is more remarkable, productive of more perfect work than that of sacred eloquence. There is no parallel among Christian nations to what France then exhibited — a school of sacred orators so lofty and finished and on the whole so profound that long after the devout had forgotten their efforts as sermons, unbelievers remembered them as literature. The Greek Fathers were not the only source of this excellence, of course; their

THE GREEK FATHERS

own oratorical works as literary masterpieces are inferior, but they had a large, direct, and acknowledged share in what the French genius here accomplished. The great originality of Bossuet, the unique fact offered in partial explanation of his unique achievement is the union in him of "the two antiquities," the union of our pagan and Christian inheritances in a mind that could absorb both as both had not been absorbed before. Greatest of pulpit orators and source of an eloquence that somehow survives the magic of its master's personality, preceptor of the Dauphin in an age of absolutism, defender of the Gallican faith, Bossuet out of the fullness of unrivalled authority insisted that in the formation of sacred orators the Scriptures and the Fathers come first. We know that Athanasius and Basil and Irenaeus cut deep grooves in his eager mind; we have elsewhere seen how St. Gregory of Nazianzus could shape the cast of one of his perorations. It is to Chrysostom among the Greek Fathers, however, to whom he is most devoted. Only St. Augustine among all the Fathers could compel his equal attention. And Bossuet never ceased to read and imitate and recommend the Golden Mouth of Antioch.

XVIITH AND XVIIITH CENTURIES

In this he was but accentuating the preference of his ecclesiastical contemporaries. St. Vincent de Paul, a center of influence from his far-reaching clerical reforms, was holding up St. Chrysostom to the emulation of popular preachers. M. Tronson of St. Sulpice, with the opportunities for detailed and penetrating guidance peculiar to a Sulpician director, had promoted the study of Chrysostom among penitents of whom Fénelon was one. Bourdaloue was a generous paraphraser of Chrysostom's thought.

Jacques Bénige Bossuet was only the greatest of an oratorical pleiad to which Bourdaloue, Fénelon, Mascaron, and Massilon gave lustre and which had a wide succession of imitators in Western Europe long after the last of them was dead. If the French language is the most perfect instrument of modern prose expression, some of its most perfect pages belong to that sacred eloquence of Louis XIV's reign, when the Greek Fathers, and especially St. Chrysostom, were nourishing its finest exemplars.

After the barren days of Elizabeth, there was a revival of Greek studies in England that issued at the close of the century in the epochal career of Bentley. One of the greatest names,

THE GREEK FATHERS

meanwhile, is that of Sir Henry Savile and the greatest single achievement, his edition of Chrysostom. It was published at Eton in 1612, the first work of learning on a grand scale ever to come forth from England. It had enlisted the ripest years of Savile's scholarly life, a large part of his fortune, and the labors of a group of coadjutors who gained fame from their coöperation. It surpassed by its display of erudition all previous English scholarship and by the magnificence of its execution all previous English book-making. Despite the high price that had to be charged for it even after Savile's generous subventions, copies of the edition were already scarce within thirty years of his death. Thus could Chrysostom command lavish attention within and without the circles of theology in a century which beyond the field of the Fathers was feeble and uncertain in its Hellenism.

The dehellenizing tendencies of the seventeenth century are accentuated through most of the eighteenth. Only in the later years of the century does an Hellenic revival begin. Further removed from Renaissance enthusiasm than the epoch of Louis XIV, heir to the declared independence of that epoch's dominating

Cartesianism, emboldened by achievements of its own that seemed warrant for such independence, the new century has currents peculiar to itself that carry it still further from Hellenism. It is the century of the Enlightenment, the Encyclopédie; of Montesquieu, Voltaire, the Revolution. All of the past that survives into the present has to pass before its judgment-seat — to be evaluated by the purely arbitrary standards of an age engrossed in itself. A disinterested pursuit of the beautiful had meant much hitherto for antiquity even among the least antiquarian spirits. That motive now is lost in the spectacle of native achievement and in the all-absorbing, impatient pursuit of social and civil reform. Latin antiquity suffers therefore in the land of its cultural descendants and Greek antiquity suffers more because of its remoter cultural affinity.

There was a feeble reflection of Hellenism in the century's earlier literature. Some distinctly Hellenic traits filtered through Latin and French into English, into the " classical " school of Pope. The sacred eloquence of France lived on for a decade or two until its great audiences dissolved among the theories of the Enlightenment. Productive classical scholarship through most of the eighteenth century was predominantly Latin scholarship outside of Holland and Germany. Even the great name of Bentley stands more for promise than achievement and his immortal *Dissertation on Aesop and Phalaris* bore its richest fruit on the Continent. The schools of the century meanwhile kept what humanism they had inherited, imparting it, as a whole, neither worse nor better than had the schools of Le Grand Siècle.

The ecclesiastical scholarship of the preceding epoch finds echo despite the Enlightenment, and the early age of the Church is explored for the sake of knowledge and controversy. From England Archbishop Potter is remembered for his edition of Clement of Alexandria, and in France there is no dearth of Greek patristic scholarship. The Benedictine monks of the Congregation of St. Maur continue their magnificent labors and the Apologists, Irenaeus, Origen, Basil, Cyril of Jerusalem, Gregory of Nazianzus (in part) are given to the world in the editions still most frequently cited. The greatest name in the Congregation after that of Dom Mabillon and one of the greatest of all the Hellenists whom the West has produced thus far is Dom Bernard du Montfaucon, founder

XVIITH AND XVIIITH CENTURIES

of Greek Paleography and promoter of French archeology. Through him Athanasius and the *Hexapla* of Origen receive a careful editing and St. Chrysostom appears in thirteen folios to the glory of French scholarship.

During the later years of the century there is a new stirring of Hellenic waters, a general revival of interest outside patristic circles and outside the non-patristic researches of Holland and Germany. Voyages being made to Greece and the growing finds of archeology hasten the return to Hellenic studies. There is still that innocence of objective historicity so characteristic of the preceding decades, but an effort is being made at any rate to get at the historical connection of things, and through the literature of Western Europe the Romantic Movement is sweeping, with its reversion to Hellenism, in Goethe and Schiller and Chénier and Collins, and, later on, in Keats and Shelley. It has nothing to do directly with the Greek Fathers save for the solitary instance of Goethe, but it heralds that more expansive, receptive era in which the Greek Fathers finally find place unchallenged, an era which finally becomes objective enough to see in them another manifestation of Hellenism.

VII. THE NINETEENTH CENTURY

THE nineteenth century, it must be said for any movement or discipline which it fostered, was preeminently the age of history. The Romantic Movement looked to the past and re-created the past in love. The Critical Movement looked to the past and tried to re-create it objectively. The spirit of reform, social and intellectual, was inherited from the eighteenth century, but eager, after the collapse of the French Revolution, to learn all that the past could tell it. It was a religious century in some of its aspects and it was very irreverent in others. But even irreverent it looked to the past sobered by a sense of history, suspecting that a thread of continuity ran through the story of mankind and then convinced of the fact by its own extensions of the ancient concept of Evolution. Neither its loves nor hates could afford excesses in the manner of the Magdeburg Centuriators and the later polemics of the century were fought in the full light of all known facts. The religious spirit turned back to the Fathers in a time so reminiscent and the secular spirit came at last to approach them with a sympathy that gave insight.

In 1795 Friedrich August Wolf published his " Prolegomena to Homer " and thereby contributed more than any other man to the launching of the Critical Movement. It was only late in the nineteenth century that its effects were fully felt and the Greek Fathers enjoyed that all-inclusiveness which Wolf made Philology's ideal. Meanwhile a few creative scholars [35] included them in their studies and the Romantic Movement and religious interests were gaining them perusal. It was not a very extensive use, though important for its contacts. Greek on the whole was faring better than in any modern period. The traditional predominance of Latin in the schools was being modified in its favor. The poets of the Romantic Movement reflected Greek more than Latin Classicism. For the Greek Fathers themselves the prejudices of centuries were being shaken — the pre-judgments against post-classical Greek still lingering in a Latin civilization, the traces of ancient estrangements with their dimly remembered causes, the specific prejudice against Byzantium, where the Greek Fathers had been in honor, the anti-religious bias bequeathed directly by the Enlightenment — all these obstacles needed such solvents as Romanticism could furnish plus the new light thrown by archeology and criticism on dark corners of the Western mind.

For the Greek Fathers, as for its intellectual side generally, the century divides roughly into halves. The first half is a kind of preparatory period for the intense activity of the second, it is getting rid of obstacles and ready for work unimpeded. The earlier decades are therefore sometimes called the Pre-critical Period, not because the critical spirit was not then a mighty factor but because other factors were then a force which later receded in power. There is little productive patristic scholarship during these earlier years, but beginnings are made, secular and clerical, which explain the later industry.

In 1802 Chateaubriand published *La génie du Christianisme* in full and the religious temper of Romanticism so vague heretofore became in large measure specifically Christian. In the strange compound of his gorgeous book Chateaubriand held up to lavish admiration the literature of the Latin Fathers. It was one of the cardinal works of the century — an enormous event in many fields of interest. Through it the heritage of irreligiosity began to lose its vogue. The Ages of Faith arose into favor, receiving a kindlier treatment. It inaugurated currents which finally overtook the Fathers — Greek as well as Latin.

In Germany meanwhile the Jew Neander did memorable work for them. Converted to Christianity, he became devoted to patristic writings in a more solid, informed way than Chateaubriand. His doctoral dissertation treated of Clement of Alexandria, and one of his latest monographs, of St. Chrysostom. Called to the University of Berlin during the later years of his life, he spread his patristic enthusiasm from that seat of influence. He was probably the first German Protestant who knew the Fathers well and something of his spirit reached America through the translation of his unfinished "Church History."

Contemporary with these events on the Continent, and in essence Romantic too, arose the Oxford Movement in England — the effort to win for the Anglican Church after a century and more of Latitudinarianism the security seen by devoted souls in its traditional theological position — oneness in all things essential with the Catholic church of the Fathers. The divines of Tudor and Caroline days had not always understood the Fathers, of course, but they had imposed them nevertheless as the basis of theology. And now in the nineteenth century when the privileges of Establishment were threatened, when a complexity of causes within and without was hurrying it on to a crisis, earnest souls in Oxford revived the Caroline method that a church patristic in practice might survive its own decay and a church patristic in lineage and doctrine might survive the Age of History.

The Greek Fathers, inevitably, had a large place in the Movement. We can see from the letters of Newman [36] how constantly and carefully he read them and how much they occupied the attention of sympathetic correspondents. Many of these writings were released to Englishmen dubious of their Greek by the *Oxford Library of the Fathers*,[37] as it is more briefly called, which Keble, Newman, and Pusey inaugurated in 1838. Most of the important doctrinal works of the Fathers — of Basil, the Gregories, Theodoret, John of

Damascus for instance — were never reached, but of the Library's forty-eight numbers, about half are devoted to the Greek Fathers and about one-third to Chrysostom alone. Athanasius and Justin and Irenaeus were also represented and other Greek Fathers were being prepared when publication had to cease. Devoted almost exclusively to fourth-century writers because of Pusey's conviction of their superiority and undoubted Catholicity, the inclusion of Justin and Irenaeus is significant of the trend to earlier writings so characteristic of the second half of the century. St. Chrysostom's *Homilies* on the *Epistles* did much to mould the thought of Anglican clergymen in the middle years of the century and through them were of effect on Anglican congregations. St. Basil's *Epistle to Diodorus* (Ep. 160) became famous and effective in discussions concerning English marriage-laws current in the 'Forties. The Movement as a whole, however, had no reading public, Newman alone commanding such a following during his Anglican years. Its influence was not a mighty one on extra-theological literature except for a certain austerity in prose from what it contributed to the temper of the times. But it gave to the Greek Fathers

THE GREEK FATHERS

a place in history, theology, and philology in England which the more comprehensive scholarship of a later day has only served to strengthen.

The presence of Irenaeus and Origen in the *Oxford Library of the Fathers* was at one with the growing importance of all Ante-Nicene writers in the consciousness of the later nineteenth century. Until now the attempts to edit them had been isolated and sporadic; attempts that may now seem important from the quality of minds attracted — Grosseteste, Erasmus, Potter — but that were isolated attempts nevertheless — exceptions to the convenient phrase " Greek Fathers," by no means embarrassing, though that phrase be limited to the Fathers of the Golden Age and be used of the Greek Patristic in the West from the fourth to the eighteenth centuries. Through patrological collections the works of the earlier Fathers were increasingly available from the time of the High Renaissance, but their rôle continued a minor rôle until the radical theology of Tübingen compelled anxious searching of their testimony.

The tenets of the School of Tübingen have for the most part passed into desuetude but the impulse they gave the study of the Fathers is still fecund, a century and more after F. C. Baur began to lecture at Tübingen University. He applied the Hegelian version of natural development to the Ante-Nicene Church. He thereby drove out the supernatural from the story of Christian origins. The wide, even popular attention which his views received because of their attacks on New Testament testimony, their underlying unison with evolutionary thought so favored at the time, the vast erudition which he enlisted in defense of his position, the efforts of distinguished disciples, particularly the *Das Leben Jesu* of Strauss, challenged the researches of orthodox scholars as they had not been challenged before and the nineteenth century rang with learned battles. The whole patristic field was thus abruptly opened to investigations still widening and deepening.

In the same years as Strauss' *Das Leben Jesu* and from the Catholic section of the same University of Tübingen, the celebrated "Symbolik" of Möhler was distracting the Protestant world. It was a study of dogmatic differences between Catholics and Protestants and aimed to show from the Fathers how different was Protestantism from the teachings of the Patristic Church. It gave further impetus to the study of the Fathers, of the history of dogma, and of the church. Möhler was also the author of a powerful polemic, *Athanasius and the Church of His Time,* and of a large work on Patrology covering the first three centuries. After the publication of the *Symbolik* Möhler went to Munich to join the famous theological group made illustrious by Döllinger, Hefele, and Görres — all of whom were vastly read in the Fathers and were channels through whom the Fathers again enriched the West.

George Eliot translated the *Das Leben Jesu* into English in 1846 and thus accentuated the orthodox misgivings which the physical sciences were breeding. The Established Church had lost the most powerful advocate of traditional theology during the previous year in the secession of Newman. Huxley and Matthew Arnold were leading a bold frontal attack with a raillery which multitudes could understand. Orthodox scholarship stood thus in fierce, unequal conflict until Westcott and Hort and Lightfoot reached their maturity. In the last decades of the century their work on Christian origins compelled even orthodox respect, and from their Alma Mater, Cambridge, there still goes forth patristic work [38] that does honor to Lightfoot and his labors on the Apostolic Fathers.

In 1836 the Abbey of Solesmes in France was formally reopened by Dom Guéranger and devoted itself to research on ritual and the Early Church. It thus early in the century laid the foundations of a reputation which in monastic and liturgical studies now reaches around the earth. Not the least of its claims to universal gratitude is the aid it gave to the Abbé Migne for his great patrological collections.

The Abbé Migne, like the Abbé de Saint-Pierre so famous in the History of Pedagogy, was a dreamer of prodigious enterprises, but thanks to his extraordinary capacity for organization and execution and to his faculty for finding competent advisers, his dreams had profitable issue. He founded at Petit-Montrouge near Paris a huge printing establishment, dedicated to the dissemination of the important theological works of all periods. Many valuable collections were thus made and, selling for a moderate price, attained to wide circulation. Later times remember him chiefly (and ought to remember Solesmes) for the near four hundred volumes of the *Patrologiae Cursus Completus,* which proceeded from his presses over a period of years from 1844. Despite the many defects inevitable in so vast an enterprise and despite the less extensive and more accurate works which now in part supplant it, it is still an indispensable instrument for extended patristic researches. Due to the generosity and energy of Migne and the erudition of Dom (afterwards Cardinal) Pitra, whom Solesmes loaned for the task, it includes within its covers nearly all the surviving Greek and Latin Fathers and a host of rare and pertinent studies gathered with vast effort. And given to the world so cheaply that even its huge bulk does not make its price prohibitive, it has rendered incalculable aid to the spread of patristic knowledge and influence in our time.

In the realm of textual excellence the *Greek Patrologia* of Migne is being in part replaced by the *Die griechischen christlichen Schriftsteller der ersten drei Jahrhunderte,* published by the Berlin Academy since 1897. The work was inaugurated by the man who towers above all other living scholars in mastery of the first three centuries — Adolph Harnack. Author, among other notable works, of a monumental

History of Dogma, of a *History of Christian Literature up to Eusebius*, and editor of a series, *Texte und Untersuchungen*, which is fundamental for the period which it covers, Harnack has been frankly apologetic in his purpose but indispensable, because of the flood of light he has shed upon the first three centuries, to those least in sympathy with his interpretations. He is the most eminent example of that devotion to the cult of facts, even personally distressing facts, characteristic of the contemporary investigator. In his gradual abandonment of rationalism and approach to the traditional position, which is the story of a long life of ever-outreaching knowledge, he exemplifies a new influence which the Fathers must exert from their unique historical position in Christianity, as scholarship more and more reveals them to candid minds.

In the last years of the Migne enterprise translations of Greek and Latin Fathers began to appear outside the rather restricted field of the *Oxford Library of the Fathers*. Thus in Edinburgh in 1866 the *Ante-Nicene Christian Library* began to be published under the editorship of Robertson and Donaldson, affording in its twenty-four volumes ready access to authors in the forefront of current scholarly interest. In Germany the *Bibliothek der Kirchenväter* began to be issued from 1869. In America the *Ante-Nicene Library* was re-published under the editorship of Bishop Cox and from 1886 *A Select Library of Nicene and Post-Nicene Fathers of the Christian Church,* edited by Philip Schaff, was inaugurated. Meanwhile translations of notable patristic works began to appear in many languages. "The Society for Promoting Christian Knowledge," founded in 1698, increased considerably the total of aids to the study of the Fathers outside the circles of the learned.

An interesting chapter in nineteenth century pedagogy — a kind of epilogue to all the awakened interest in the Fathers and instructive of the utmost rôle they can hope to play in the modern West, despite the efforts of some of their protagonists — is the "Gaume Controversy," so-called from the French priest who precipitated it. It was a modern version of the ancient quarrel over the use of pagan classics by Christian students. After the French Revolution there was widespread concern over the growing rationalism and materialism in society. The times of '48 served to intensify anxiety so that when the Abbé Gaume published his "Le Ver Rongeur" in 1851, his proposals gained a continental hearing. Starting from the principle that the ills of society could be cured only by substituting Christianity for paganism in education, he advocated that Christian authors, Greek and Latin, be studied to the exclusion of pagan writers in the earlier and larger part of school courses. The Jesuit, Charles Daniel, made a very able protest against Gaume's views in 1853 and a literature of controversy developed over a period of about fifteen years, Montalembert, Louis Veuillot, and Cardinal Gousset supporting the views of Gaume, while Bishop Dupanloup lead opposition. Finally after Belgium, Italy, Austria, Ireland, France, and Germany had become thoroughly aroused, Pius IX settled the dispute in the spirit of St. Basil and St. Augustine fifteen centuries before; and the Fathers, Greek and Latin, kept their traditionally minor rôle in schemata of studies, in circles most favorable to their content, and in the century more hospitable, generally, to the Greek Fathers, in the West, than any period since the days of St. Augustine.

VIII. CONCLUSION

SOMETHING of Gibbon's thesis on the fall of ancient civilization may be applied to that part of it which is the Greek Fathers. They too began to decline in the West after the Age of the Antonines, involved in the decay of Western Hellenism which was then becoming visible. Hitherto, at least from the Scipionic Age, the Hellenism of the West had been mostly a direct Hellenism, unembarrassed by diversity of tongues. Hereafter and increasingly it was to be a Hellenism of translations. Greek was fading out of the civilized West as a spoken and written language and the West, still eager for some of its riches, got them through Latin versions. Of the Greek Fathers, in fact, there was much translating in the later second century and still later, in the fourth century, there was a great translation period. And thus it has ever since been for Greek and the Greek Fathers in the Occident. Intellectual revivals have come — with always a desire for Greek as the key to priceless treasures. But

CONCLUSION

it has ever been easier to conjecture its value than to overtake it widely. The Greek Fathers have kept returning to the West in response to one motive and another, reinforcing again under some new aspect what they had given long ago, influencing the West at vital periods but always in an alien tongue, lacking the colloquial advantage they enjoyed when Marcus Aurelius reigned.

One part of Gibbon's thesis cannot be applied to the Greek Fathers. They were not in their heyday of excellence when the Antonines were ruling. The Fathers of the greatest immediate authority were a century still unborn, when the Western fate of Hellenic authors began to overtake them. For nearly three centuries after the Antonines the Greek Fathers lingered in the West, enjoying the same primacy of influence and honor as when Greek had been the Church's vernacular. And then their primacy faded before the rising authority of Augustine and their very memory was all but lost in the avalanche of barbarian invasions.

These two events are cardinal to the rôle of the Greek Fathers in Europe. Before Augustine their influence was overwhelmingly predominant, even when in its latest years it worked chiefly through translations; after Augustine it was never predominant as a new current from the East, as independent of that part of itself already lodged in the West. And the perseverance of the Empire in the East against the assaults of barbaric invaders assured to the Fathers continued preeminence where Byzantium would rule and evangelize. The final collapse of the Empire in the West was the last of a series of causes [39] dividing East from West in a cultural dualism which the Greek Fathers were the first to feel. In Graeco-Slavic Europe they have ever dominated theology and their greater names are written large across Graeco-Slavic literature. In Graeco-Latin Europe they have never recovered the leadership already doomed by the genius of Augustine before the barbarians prevailed.

Their influence has been a mighty and permanent thing despite the obscurity which so frequently attends it. One of the cardinal facts of Western civilization is the part of Christianity in it. From Classical Antiquity and Christian Antiquity we are sprung, intellectually and culturally. And one of the cardinal facts of the Christian religion is the part of Tradition in it, the extra-scriptural source of

CONCLUSION

Revelation, ancient and yet ever actual; to the majority of Christians a font of truth and to all men an historical phenomenon. And one of the cardinal facts about Tradition itself is the part of the Greek Fathers in it, that almost monopoly of leadership after Apostolic times, if rare papal pronouncements be excepted, in those early, vital, formative centuries which after-ages only elaborate. The gradual growth from the occasional and accidental and unpremeditated statement so characteristic of the Apostolic Fathers to the first attempts at philosophic defense in the Apologists of the second century, to the first signal use of Tradition against the menace of the Gnostic doctrines, to the first essays in systematic theology issuing from third-century Alexandria, to the classic expositions on the Incarnation and the Trinity in the fourth and fifth centuries and the multitude of lesser questions then touched in discursive treatises — this slowly but widely unfolding effort is chiefly a Greek achievement: of Ignatius and Justin and Tatian and Melito, Irenaeus and Clement and Origen; of Athanasius and Basil, the Gregories and Chrysostom, Theodoret, and Cyril of Alexandria. If by decree of inscrutable Providence the rôle of

THE GREEK FATHERS

these Fathers ceased here, if only the men just named in the points just named were the story of Christian Hellenism, that rôle were still an enormous fact in the intellectual life of the West because of solutions given to vital problems in a living and powerful tradition.

Beyond the expositions which they gave in their own time of the deposit of the faith, certain of the Greek Fathers did work allied to theology caught up into the traditions of the West. Thus the reorganization of Greek philosophy as an instrument of Christianity, the appropriation of its method minus its self-sufficient purpose, the vindication of love of God rather than knowledge as the highest activity of the soul — this mighty and delicate philosophic task, so preliminary to the Scholasticism of medieval and modern times, was initiated and in its outlines executed by Greek Fathers, by Justin and Origen and Clement of Alexandria and others. In the field of exegesis the biblical studies of medieval Latins are chiefly echoes of Greek predecessors. And even in the eighth and ninth centuries, when Greek was so rare in the West, the commentaries of Bede, Rhabanus Maurus, of Walafried Strabo are compilations that have their

CONCLUSION

largest source in the Greek Fathers, and in Origen above all others. And the part played by symbolism and allegory in the life of the Middle Ages has its roots again in Alexandria and the exegesis favored there. The opposite school of Antioch, with its grammatico-historical method, in the works of Chrysostom nourishes after-ages down to the present day. The Greeks showed on the whole more readiness than the Latins in meeting the problem presented by the need of secular learning despite its attendant dangers. The insistence upon religion as the core of education, of the life beyond the grave as its highest aim; the emphasis on the spiritual rather than on the intellectual in man and the necessary corollary that education is for all men rather than the chosen few — these guiding principles ever characteristic of Christianity in the field of education were the pioneer work of Clement and Basil and Gregory of Nazianzus and Chrysostom. And if we recall Eusebius' major place in the History of Historiography, the posthumous career of Nazianzus and Chrysostom in the field of sacred eloquence, the work of Athanasius and Basil in the beginnings of monasticism, the rôles of Gregory of Nyssa and the

THE GREEK FATHERS

Areopagite in the wide fields of Mysticism, if we repeat the names of Ambrose, Hilary, Jerome, Augustine, John Cassian, and Cassiodorus; Gregory the Great, Rhabanus Maurus, Alcuin, and Hincmar of Rheims; Scotus Eriügena, Robert Grosseteste, Peter Lombard, Hugh of St. Victor; Alexander of Hales, Albert the Great, St. Thomas, and St. Bonaventure; Erasmus, Melanchthon, Oecolampadius, Zwingli, and St. Francis de Sales; Bossuet, Bourdaloue, Fénelon, Savile, the St. Maur Congregation, and Goethe; Neander, Newman, Boeckh, von Ranke, Pusey, Keble and Baur; Lightfoot, Harnack, Armitage Robinson, Batiffol, Bardenhewer, and Puech, if we review their careers in their patristic contacts and as centers of far-reaching influence, we know something of the fact of the Greek Patristic in the life of the spirit in the West.

The West rediscovers but tardily this part of its traditions and even in the expansive nineteenth century was in the grip of old prejudices against the Greek Fathers — of scientists against theology, of Puritans against Roman Catholics and Anglicans, of historical scholarship against Byzantium, of Attic and Ciceronian enthusiasts against all later epochs of antiquity. There is the story of so competent a classicist as Gaisford, during his Regius Professorship days, showing a friend through Christ Church Library. After a long pause over the treasures of pagan classics which the Library shelters, he hurried by the volumes of the Fathers murmuring "sad rubbish."[40] And there was a Puritan contemporary of Gaisford who summed up the convictions of his kind by branding the works of the Fathers as "the stinking puddles of tradition."[41] These incidents are not peculiar to an "insularity of British scholarship" of which critics used to complain. They are part of an insularity of which scholarship generally was guilty in the century which called itself the Age of History. The great History of Greek Literature by Christ reflects this insularity in its earlier editions. The corresponding Latin work of Professor Schanz was bitterly attacked for a time because of its inclusion of Latin Fathers within its scope. The celebrated school of Roman Law founded by Sevigny in the first decades of the nineteenth century was violently distressed at the suggestion that its subject had patristic phases, now recognized as of primary and obvious import.[42] In 1877 Professor

Gildersleeve published an edition of *The Apologies of Justin Martyr* in an effort to stir up patristic studies that was as generous and brilliant as it was futile.[43] Ulrich von Wilamowitz-Moellendorf is the author of a spirited passage on the " disgrace " of Modern Philology in its neglect of Gregory of Nazianzus as a poet.[44] The obscurantists of the Ancient Church who protested the study of the pagan classics have their counterparts in Modern Philology, who protest the study of the Fathers.

The present age is not a part of history but it seems to realize more fully in its first quarter century that Wolfian ideal which the preceding century professed — and realized so magnificently in Mommsen. It is anxious to know in its historical queries all that the past can tell it that it may see all epochs in their environment. In this is a new hope for the Greek Fathers. It will not resurrect them as literature; they will never again have the wide vogue that was theirs among the educated in early Christian circles; not even their sermons could have wide appeal in their strange sophistic devices; but it does give them a new career that they are the sources of secular historians, adding the historical motive to the theological and polemical

CONCLUSION

in the scope of their contemporary influence. And it does give them a place of honor along side of other venerated and little read literature, commensurate with their place in the living traditions of Europe. In this spirit they are being included in *The Loeb Classical Library,* in the French *Collection Guillaume Budé,* and in *Our Debt to Greece and Rome,* which in this little volume would convince the "general reader" that something besides religious conservatism and squatter's rights keeps the Migne on our library shelves.

NOTES AND BIBLIOGRAPHY

NOTES*

1. Maximus Confessor, d. 662, is a striking exception on the score of originality, but what he contributed to the West reached it for the most part through the summary of St. John of Damascus.

2. The term in usage permits of a much larger extension; into the Middle Ages in fact, as Migne so conceived it.

3. Pope St. Clement, St. Ignatius of Antioch, St. Polycarp, Pseudo-Barnabas, the Didache, the Second Epistle of Clement, the Shepherd of Hermas, Papias, The Apostles' Creed.

4. Quadratus, Aristo of Pella, Miltiades, Apollinaris of Hierapolis, Melito, Aristides, Justin Martyr, Tatian, Athenagoras, Theophilus, The Epistle to Diognetus, Hermias.

5. *Opera,* ed. Basel, 1558, 99. Cf. *ibid.* IX. 75.

6. Cf. C. Bigg, *op. cit.,* 351 ff.

7. The most plausible account of this vexed question I found in P. Pourrat, *La spiritualité chrétienne. Des origines de l'Église au moyen âge,* Paris, 1918.

8. St. Augustine, *The Confessions,* Bk. VIII. ch. 6–7. (Watts' Translation).

9. J. David, "Antoine," in *Dictionnaire d'Histoire et de Géographie ecclésiastique,* III. 732-3 (1924).

10. Cf. J. Pargoire, "Basile de Césarée," in Fernand Cabrol's *Dictionnaire d'Archéologie chrétienne et de Liturgie,* II. 501 ff. (1910); W. K. L. Clark, *St. Basil the Great, A Study in Monasticism,* Cambridge, 1913; E. F. Morison, *St. Basil and His Rule,* Oxford, 1912, and especially Dom

* *Op. cit.* refers to works cited in the Bibliography, 163–167.

Cuthbert Butler, *Sancti Benedicti Regula Monachorum*, Freiburg-i-B., 1912, 179, where sixteen parallels between Benedict and Basil are indicated.

11. Cf. P. de Labriolle, *Histoire de la Littérature latine chrétienne*,[2] Paris, 1924, 34–36; Carl Weyman, *Historisches Jahrbuch*, XXX, 287 ff. (1909).

12. The following details, among others, of the second part of Goethe's *Faust* have their counterpart in St. Gregory's *Vita Mosis:* the ascent to the high mountain in the morning; the bath of purification; the contemplation of the light of the rising sun, which appears to the beholder as darkness; the persistent desire for beauty; the question of what life is — all in the opening scene of Part II: besides, details in the sleep of Faust, in the monologue at the appearance of the sun, in the changing of divine light into darkness. Cf. Konrad Burdach, *Sitzungsberichte der Berliner Akademie der Wissenschaft*, 1912, 397 ff.; 786 ff.

13. "For as Gregory Nazianzen of revered memory hath taught long before us" etc., from Prologue to Part III of the *Regula Pastoralis*. Cf. F. H. Didden, *Gregory the Great*, London, 1905, I. 229, 235.

14. The Epigrams were translated by Thomas Drant and published from London in 1568. The Epitaphs were translated by H. S. Boyd in his *Gregorius Nazianzenus, Tributes to the Dead*, London, 1826. The paraphrases of Newman may be found in Newman's *Church of the Fathers*, ch. 3, 4.

15. Cf. *op. cit.*, 214 ff.

16. *Paradiso*, canto 28, v. 130., Cary's translation. Cf. also *ibid.*, canto 10, v. 115.

17. Bishop Westcott in Smith and Wace's *Dictionary of Christian Biography*, s.v. "Dionysius" I. 847–8, London, 1877.

18. All the ante-Nicene figures except Origen seem to be ignored, and Origen is named only to be attacked. Cf. Krumbacher, *op. cit.*, 70.

19. A good summary in Jordan, *op. cit.*, 435 ff.

NOTES

20. Cf. De Labriolle, *op. cit.*, 485, ft. n. 1.
21. Cf. S. Angus, *The Sources of the First Ten Books of the De Civitate Dei of St. Augustine*, Princeton, 1906, 236 ff.
22. Cf. *De Civitate Dei*, XVI. 16; XVIII. 8, 10, 25, 31, where Augustine refers specifically to the *Chronica*.
23. e. g. Max Manitius, "Philologisches aus Alten Bibliothekskatalogen (bis 1300)," in *Rheinisches Museum*, XLVII (Supplementband, 1–152), (1892).
24. Origen and Basil, along with Eusebius, are found among the Greek patristic traces of the ninth-century West. Cf. A. Souter, "Basil and Origen as Sources of Sedulius Scotus," in *Journal of Theological Studies*, XVIII. 184–228 (1916–1917).
25. For a review of the question, cf. Sandys, *op. cit.*, I. 583–4.
26. Cf. Roger Bacon, *Compendium Studii Philosophiae*, ch. 8, *Opera Quaedam Hactenus Inedita*, vol. I. ed. by J. S. Brewer, London, 1859, 474. Translation from *Cambridge Modern History*, I. 585.
27. *Erasmi Opera Omnia, Tomus Tertius qui complectitur Epistolas*, ed. by Leclerc, Lugduni Batavorum, 1703, ep. 583, 751.
28. Cf. P. L. J. Villey-Desmeserets, *Les sources et l'évolution des essais de Montaigne*, 2 vols., Paris, 1908, I. 51–270.
29. Cf. Grisar, *op. cit.*, I. 320.
30. Cf. Grisar, *op. cit.*, I. 181.
31. Cf. Grisar, *op. cit.*, IV. 411, 412.
32. Cf. Grisar, *op. cit.*, IV. 335.
33. Cf. Willmann-Kirsch, *op. cit.*, I. 254.
34. Cf. beginnings of his treatise *L'Éducation des Filles*.
35. e. g. August Boeckh, who made of Classical Philology an historical science, and Leopold von Ranke. Cf. Johannes Naegele, "Johannes Chrysostomos und sein Verhältnis zum Hellenismus," in *Byzantinische Zeitschrift*, XIII. 73 ff. (1904).
36. Cf. Anne Mozley, *Letters and Correspondence of*

THE GREEK FATHERS

J. H. Newman During His Life in the English Church, London, 1891, I. 212, 251; II. 119, 122, 126, 292.

37. *The Fathers of the Holy Catholic Church Anterior to the Division of East and West,* 43 vols., 1838–1885. (43 vols. and five unattached numbers.)

38. e. g. *Texts and Studies,* edited by J. Armitage Robinson, 1896 ff., and *Cambridge Patristic Texts,* edited by A. J. Mason, 1899 ff.

39. Cf. F. Lot, *Le fin du monde antique et la début du moyen âge,* Paris, 1927, 257 ff.

40. Cf. T. Mozley, *Reminiscences of Oriel College and the Oxford Movement,* 2 vols., 1882, I. 356.

41. Cf. Liddon's *Life of Pusey,* I. 434.

42. Salvatore Riccobono, "The Evolution of Roman Law," ch. I., in lectures as yet unpublished.

43. B. L. Gildersleeve, *The Apologies of Justin Martyr,* New York, 1877.

44. *Op. cit.* 218. "This same Gregory is the most prolific and most noteworthy poet of this period. It is a disgrace that philologists have not yet brought out a single tolerably readable edition of his poems. If he were not a church-father, but some trite poetaster spinning out the hackneyed materials of mythology, like Quintus, or even a Latin poet, like Silius, he long since would have found an editor."

BIBLIOGRAPHY

Of over twelve hundred works, monographs, articles known by me to be pertinent to a study of this kind, I offer the following selection with some misgivings as to its representative character. Monographs pertinent to a single point only are mentioned in the notes.

GENERAL

BATIFFOL, P., *Anciennes Littératures chrétiennes: La Littérature grecque.* Paris, 1897.
BARDENHEWER, O., *Geschichte der altkirchlichen Litteratur,*[2] 4 vols. Freiburg-im-Breisgau, 1912–1924.
BARDENHEWER, O., *Patrologie.*[3] Freiburg-im-Breisgau, 1910. Translated from the 2nd German edition with augmented bibliographies by T. J. Shahan, St. Louis, 1908.
BAUMGARTNER, A., S. J., *Geschichte der Weltliteratur;* vol. III, *Die griechische und lateinische Literatur des klassischen Altertums.* Freiburg-im-Breisgau, 1900–1911.
CHRIST, W. VON, *Griechische Literaturgeschichte,*[6] IIer Teil, umbgt. von Schmid und Stählin. München, 1924.
CROISET, A. and M., *Histoire de la Littérature grecque,* vol. v. Paris, 1899.
FISHER, GEORGE P., *History of Christian Doctrine.* New York, (1896) 1909.
HARNACK, A., *Geschichte der altchristlichen Literatur bis Eusebius,* vol. I in collaboration with E. Preuschen. Leipzig, 1893; vol. II. Leipzig, 1897–1904.
HESSEN, J., *Patristische und scholastische Philosophie.* Breslau, 1922.
KRUMBACHER, K., *Geschichte der byzantinischen Literatur.*[2] München, 1897.

THE GREEK FATHERS

Leigh-Bennett, E., *Handbook of the Early Christian Fathers*. London, 1920.
Norden, E., *Die Antike Kunstprosa*, 4th reprint, 2 vols. Leipzig, 1923.
Puech, A., *Histoire de la Littérature grecque chrétienne*, vols. I, II. Paris, 1928.
Sandys, Sir J. E., *A History of Classical Scholarship*, vol. I (3rd ed.), II, III. Cambridge, 1906–1921.
Tixeront, J., *Histoire des Dogmes*, 3 vols. Paris, 1906–1912. Translated by H. L. B., 3 vols. St. Louis, 1910–1916.
Ueberweg, F., *Grundriss der Geschichte der Philosophie*, Part I, *Die Philosophie des Altertums*,[12] hrsg. von K. Praechter. Berlin, 1926; Part II, *Die patristische und scholastische Philosophie*,[11] hrsg. von B. Geyer. Berlin, 1928.
Wilamowitz-Moellendorff, U. von, "Die griechische Literatur des Altertums," in *Die Kultur der Gegenwart*, Part I, Section 8 E, Oströmische Periode, I, Das christliche Ostrom. Berlin und Leipzig, 1912.
Willmann, Otto, *Didaktik als Bildungslehre nach ihren Beziehungen zur Socialforschung und zur Geschichte der Bildung*.[4] Braunschweig, 1909. Translation of Felix M. Kirsch, O. M. Cap., 2 vols. Beatty, Pa., 1921–1922.

CHAPTER I

Bevan, Edwynn, *Hellenism and Christianity*, ch. IV. London, 1921.
Croiset, M., *La Civilisation hellénique*. Paris, 1922. Translation by Paul B. Thomas, New York, 1925.
Jordan, H., *Geschichte der altkirchlichen Literatur*. Leipzig, 1911.
Wendland, P., *Die hellenistisch-römische Kultur in ihren Beziehungen zu Judentum und Christentum*, 2nd and 3rd ed. Tübingen, 1912.

BIBLIOGRAPHY

CHAPTER II

BARDY, G., *Saint Athanase.*² Paris, 1914.

BAUR, DOM CHR., O. S. B., *S. Jean Chrysostome et ses œuvres dans l'histoire littéraire.* Louvain et Paris, 1907.

BIGG, C., *The Christian Platonists of Alexandria.*² Oxford, 1913.

CHASE, F. H., *Chrysostom, A Study in the History of Biblical Interpretation.* Cambridge, 1897.

DE FAYE, E. DE, *Gnostiques et Gnosticisme.*² Paris, 1925.

DE FAYE, E. DE, *Clément d'Alexandrie, Étude sur les rapports du christianisme et la philosophie grecque au IIIe siècle.*² Paris, 1906.

DE FAYE, E. DE, *Origène.* I, Paris, 1923; II, Paris, 1927.

DENIS, J., *De la philosophie d'Origène.* Paris, 1884.

GRABMANN, M., "Pseudo-Dionysius Areopagita in lateinischen Uebersetzungen des Mittelalters," in *Festgabe A. Ehrhard.* Bonn und Leipzig, 1922.

NAEGELE, A., "Johannes Chrysostomos und sein Verhältnis zum Hellenismus," in *Byzantinische Zeitschrift*, XIII. 73–113. (1904).

PRAT, F., *Origène, le théologien et l'interprète.* Paris, 1907.

PUECH, A., *Les Apologistes grecs du IIe siècle de notre ère.* Paris, 1912.

PUECH, A., *S. Jean Chrysostome et les mœurs de son temps.* Paris, 1891.

PUECH, A., *S. Jean Chrysostome.*⁵ Paris, 1905. Translated by Mildred Partridge, 2nd ed. London, 1917.

ROLT, C. E., *Dionysius the Areopagite, On the Divine Names and the Mystical Theology*, (S. P. C. K.). London, 1920.

SHOTWELL, J. T., *An Introduction to the History of History*, chs. XXV–XXVI. New York, 1922.

WESTCOTT, B. F., *The Religious Thought of the West*, 142 ff.; 194 ff. London and New York, 1891.

THE GREEK FATHERS

CHAPTER III

ANGUS, S., *The Sources of the First Ten Books of Augustine's De Civitate Dei.* Princeton, 1906.

DE LABRIOLLE, P. DE, *Histoire de la littérature latine chrétienne.*² Paris, 1924. Translation (1st. ed.) by H. Wilson. London, 1924.

HESSEN, JOHANNES, *Augustinus und seine Bedeutung für die Gegenwart.* Stuttgart, 1924.

RAND, E. K., *The Founders of the Middle Ages.* Cambridge, 1928.

CHAPTER IV

BOISSONADE, P., *Le travail dans l'Europe chrétienne au moyen âge.* Paris, 1921. Translation by E. Power, London and New York, 1927, Book I.

BREHIÈR, L., "Normal Relations Between East and West Before the Schism of the XI Century," in *Constructive Quarterly,* IV. 645 ff. (1916).

BYRNE, E. H., *The Genoese Colonies in Syria, The Crusades and Other Essays Presented to Dana C. Munro,* edited by L. J. Paetow, 139 ff. New York, 1928.

HASKINS, C. H., *The Renaissance of the Twelfth Century.* Cambridge, 1927.

HASKINS, C. H., "The Spread of Ideas in the Middle Ages," in *Speculum,* I. 19 ff. (1926).

HASKINS, C. H., *Studies in the History of Medieval Science,* ch. II. Cambridge, 1924.

HUMBERT, A., *Les origines de la théologie moderne,* vol. I. Paris, 1911.

JANSSEN, J., *History of the German People at the Close of the Middle Ages,* Translation of Mitchell and Christie, vol. I, bk. I. St. Louis, n. d.

LOOMIS, L. R., *Medieval Hellenism.* Lancaster, 1906.

STEINACKER, H., "Die römische Kirche und die griechischen Sprachkenntnisse des Frühmittelalters," in *Festschrift für Theodor Gomperz,* 324 ff. Wien, 1902.

BIBLIOGRAPHY

TAYLOR, H. O., *The Classical Heritage of the Middle Ages.* New York, 1901.
TRAUBE, L., LEHMANN, P., *Einleitung in die lateinische Philologie des Mittelalters,* 82 ff. München, 1911.

CHAPTER V

BYWATER, I., *Four Centuries of Greek Learning in England.* Oxford, 1919.
GASQUET, F. A., *The Eve of the Reformation.* London, 1900.
HALLAM, HENRY, *Introduction to the Literature of Europe,* etc., vols. I, II. London, 1838–1839.
HUMBERT, A., *Les origines de la théologie moderne,* vol. I. Paris, 1911.
JANSSEN, J., *History of the German People at Close of the Middle Ages,* Translation of Mitchell and Christie, vol. III, bk. 5, ch. I. St. Louis, 1900.

CHAPTER VI

BOULVE, LÉON, *De l'Hellénisme chez Fénelon.* Paris, 1897.
EGGER, E., *L'Hellénisme en France,* vols. I, II. Paris, 1869.
FLOYET, M., *Études sur la vie de Bossuet,* vol. II, 521. Paris, 1855.
HALLAM, HENRY, *Introduction to the Literature of Europe,* etc., vol. II. London, 1838–1839.

CHAPTER VII

CHURCH, R. W., *The Oxford Movement, Twelve Years, 1833–1845.* London, 1900.
DUBLIN REVIEW, XXXIII, 321–336; VII (New Series) 200–228, on the Gaume Controversy.
GOOCH, G. P., *History and Historians in the Nineteenth Century.* London, 1928.
LIDDON, H. P., *Life of Pusey,* vols. I–IV. London, 1893–1897.
THUREAU-DANGIN, P., *Le Renaissance Catholique en Angleterre.* Paris, 1912.

Our Debt to Greece and Rome

AUTHORS AND TITLES

HOMER. *John A. Scott.*
SAPPHO. *David M. Robinson.*
EURIPIDES. *F. L. Lucas.*
ARISTOPHANES. *Louis E. Lord.*
DEMOSTHENES. *Charles D. Adams.*
THE POETICS OF ARISTOTLE. *Lane Cooper.*
GREEK RHETORIC AND LITERARY CRITICISM. *W. Rhys Roberts.*
LUCIAN. *Francis G. Allinson.*
CICERO AND HIS INFLUENCE. *John C. Rolfe.*
CATULLUS. *Karl P. Harrington.*
LUCRETIUS AND HIS INFLUENCE. *George Depue Hadzsits.*
OVID. *Edward Kennard Rand.*
HORACE. *Grant Showerman.*
VIRGIL. *John William Mackail.*
SENECA THE PHILOSOPHER. *Richard Mott Gummere.*
APULEIUS. *Elizabeth Hazelton Haight.*
MARTIAL. *Paul Nixon.*
PLATONISM. *Alfred Edward Taylor.*
ARISTOTELIANISM. *John L. Stocks.*
STOICISM. *Robert Mark Wenley.*
LANGUAGE AND PHILOLOGY. *Roland G. Kent.*

AUTHORS AND TITLES

AESCHYLUS AND SOPHOCLES. *J. T. Sheppard.*
GREEK RELIGION. *Walter Woodburn Hyde.*
SURVIVALS OF ROMAN RELIGION. *Gordon J. Laing.*
MYTHOLOGY. *Jane Ellen Harrison.*
ANCIENT BELIEFS IN THE IMMORTALITY OF THE SOUL. *Clifford H. Moore.*
STAGE ANTIQUITIES. *James Turney Allen.*
PLAUTUS AND TERENCE. *Gilbert Norwood.*
ROMAN POLITICS. *Frank Frost Abbott.*
PSYCHOLOGY, ANCIENT AND MODERN. *G. S. Brett.*
ANCIENT AND MODERN ROME. *Rodolfo Lanciani.*
WARFARE BY LAND AND SEA. *Eugene S. McCartney.*
THE GREEK FATHERS. *James Marshall Campbell.*
GREEK BIOLOGY AND MEDICINE. *Henry Osborn Taylor.*
MATHEMATICS. *David Eugene Smith.*
LOVE OF NATURE AMONG THE GREEKS AND ROMANS. *H. R. Fairclough.*
ANCIENT WRITING AND ITS INFLUENCE. *B. L. Ullman.*
GREEK ART. *Arthur Fairbanks.*
ARCHITECTURE. *Alfred M. Brooks.*
ENGINEERING. *Alexander P. Gest.*
MODERN TRAITS IN OLD GREEK LIFE. *Charles Burton Gulick.*
ROMAN PRIVATE LIFE. *Walton Brooks McDaniel.*
GREEK AND ROMAN FOLKLORE. *William Reginald Halliday.*
ANCIENT EDUCATION. *J. F. Dobson.*